Why Is Welfare
So Hard to Reform?

Studies in Social Economics
TITLES PUBLISHED

STUDIES IN SOCIAL ECONOMICS

Why Is Welfare So Hard to Reform?

A Staff Paper by Henry J. Aaron

THE BROOKINGS INSTITUTION
Washington, D.C.

Copyright © 1973 by
THE BROOKINGS INSTITUTION
1775 Massachusetts Avenue, N.W., Washington, D.C. 20036

Library of Congress Cataloging in Publication Data:
Aaron, Henry J
  Why is welfare so hard to reform?

  (Studies in social economics)
  Includes bibliographical references.
  1. Public welfare—United States.
I. Title.   II. Series.
HV95.A595   361.6′0973   72-13543
ISBN 0-8157-0019-9 (pbk)

9 8 7 6 5 4 3

THE BROOKINGS INSTITUTION is an independent organization devoted to nonpartisan research, education, and publication in economics, government, foreign policy, and the social sciences generally. Its principal purposes are to aid in the development of sound public policies and to promote public understanding of issues of national importance.

The Institution was founded on December 8, 1927, to merge the activities of the Institute for Government Research, founded in 1916, the Institute of Economics, founded in 1922, and the Robert Brookings Graduate School of Economics and Government, founded in 1924.

The Board of Trustees is responsible for the general administration of the Institution, while the immediate direction of the policies, program, and staff is vested in the President, assisted by an advisory committee of the officers and staff. The by-laws of the Institution state, "It is the function of the Trustees to make possible the conduct of scientific research, and publication, under the most favorable conditions, and to safeguard the independence of the research staff in the pursuit of their studies and in the publication of the results of such studies. It is not a part of their function to determine, control, or influence the conduct of particular investigations or the conclusions reached."

The President bears final responsibility for the decision to publish a manuscript as a Brookings book or staff paper. In reaching his judgment on the competence, accuracy, and objectivity of each study, the President is advised by the director of the appropriate research program and weighs the views of a panel of expert outside readers who report to him in confidence on the quality of the work. Publication of a work signifies that it is deemed to be a competent treatment worthy of public consideration; such publication does not imply endorsement of conclusions or recommendations contained in the study.

The Institution maintains its position of neutrality on issues of public policy in order to safeguard the intellectual freedom of the staff. Hence interpretations or conclusions in Brookings publications should be understood to be solely those of the author or authors and should not be attributed to the Institution, to its trustees, officers, or other staff members, or to the organizations that support its research.

Foreword

For three years Congress and the administration have tried without success to reform welfare. A number of proposals to correct what is customarily described as "the welfare mess" have been debated, but a consensus has formed around none.

The issue of work incentives was a central dilemma in the congressional debate. How could employable adult welfare recipients be induced or compelled to accept jobs? Efforts to answer this question directed attention to the implicit marginal tax rate on earnings under the current welfare system —the amount by which an increase in earnings is offset by reductions in cash assistance, housing subsidies, food stamps, medical assistance, or other benefits, or by increases in payroll and income taxes.

This paper focuses on the problem of the cumulative marginal tax rate. It shows how the present system of benefits works and how, while it provides recipients with substantial assistance, it also confronts them with heavier effective tax rates than any other group must pay. The author examines the major proposals that have been advanced in recent years to strengthen work incentives; to broaden, increase, or reduce the geographic variation of benefits; and to restrict the scope of bureaucratic discretion. He suggests that the proposed reforms would weaken, not strengthen, incentives to work.

But there is a more basic issue: Why has it proved so difficult to design a welfare system that would make employment an attractive alternative to continued dependence on welfare assistance? The author suggests that the difficulty stems from the failure of reform efforts adequately to come to grips with the interrelatedness of the numerous assistance programs. He proposes a reformed and integrated system consisting of cash, housing, and medical assistance, designed to keep cumulative tax rates down and to provide potential workers with a strong incentive to work full time.

Henry J. Aaron is a senior fellow in the Economics Studies Program at the Brookings Institution and a member of the economics faculty at the University of Maryland. He wishes to thank Jodie T. Allen, Nelson Mc-Clung, Robert H. Haveman, Robert J. Lampman, Robert A. Levine, Robert W. Hartman, Robert D. Reischauer, Karen Davis, Gilbert Y. Steiner, Leonard Goodwin, Joseph A. Pechman, and Richard P. Nathan for reading drafts of the paper and making numerous helpful comments. Robert M. Gordon and Julia Clones provided research assistance. Katherine P. Matheson typed the manuscript. Evelyn P. Fisher checked it for statistical accuracy and Mendelle T. Berenson edited it.

This staff paper is the tenth publication in the Brookings series of Studies in Social Economics. The series presents the results of research focused on selected problems in the fields of health, education, social security, and welfare. This study was supported by a grant from the Edna McConnell Clark Foundation. The views expressed in this publication are solely those of the author, and should not be attributed to the trustees, officers, or other staff members of the Brookings Institution or to the Edna McConnell Clark Foundation.

KERMIT GORDON
President

December 1972
Washington, D.C.

Contents

Tables

Figures

Why Is Welfare So Hard to Reform?

CHAPTER ONE

Introduction

President Nixon has stated that passage of welfare reform would be the most significant domestic social legislation since enactment of social security in 1935. Many quarrel with his definition of reform, but few question the President's judgment that the existing welfare system requires extensive change. Welfare has been indicted for encouraging family dissolution, promoting illegitimacy, degrading and alienating recipients, papering over the sins of a society that generates poverty, shielding the dissolute and lazy from their just deserts, failing to support life by providing too little assistance, and fostering sloth by providing too much. Conservatives, liberals, and radicals unite in attacking the welfare system but divide over its specific faults.

Much of the controversy about the welfare system and welfare recipients rests on unresolvable ethical and philosophical differences, and some of it on persistent, if unconscious, racial and ethnic prejudice. Welfare recipients are disproportionately black, Chicano, and Puerto Rican. Adult recipients are largely deserted mothers and mothers of illegitimate children—and illegitimate children and their mothers continue to provoke antipathy. Furthermore, welfare recipients are less likely to vote than other groups, a fact well known to elected officials. As one observer noted in explaining why welfare for the aged commands greater support and generates less controversy than welfare for children and their mothers, "Perhaps the most crucial difference . . . is that the aged poor are primarily white, they vote, and they don't have illegitimate children."[1] The most basic reason why welfare reform is difficult to achieve is that welfare recipients are politically unpopular and weak, and socially set apart from the great mass of the population.[2]

Because the politics of welfare expresses various attitudes about welfare recipients and about other values, no agreement exists about what constitutes welfare reform even if cost were no object. But both costs and attitudes are implicit in the questions surrounding reform. How high should payments be set for families with no outside earnings? How rapidly should benefits be reduced as earnings rise? Who should be eligible? Should work be required of all, some, or no recipients? Who should administer the program? How much discretion should be exercised in each welfare case in setting benefits? The formation of a consensus on these questions is further hindered by ignorance and confusion about how welfare recipients and others respond to the current system, and how they would respond to the various alternatives that have been advanced. The effects of welfare on migration, desertion, and illegitimacy remain unclear.

One theme common to most critics is a belief that the present public welfare system discourages work effort. Some allege that it makes work so unprofitable and dependency so attractive that children follow the footsteps of their parents to the public dole. Many recipients have poor earnings prospects, owing to inadequate education or training, or other personal disabilities, and thus welfare payments, especially for large families, may equal or exceed full-time earnings at the minimum wage.

But that is only part of the problem. The welfare system is alleged to prevent recipients from increasing their incomes through work. Only since 1967 have most states failed to cut welfare payments dollar for dollar of earnings, and even the liberalized benefit formulas in effect since then allow recipients to keep only one-third of earnings over $360 a year; this means that a recipient who works a week at the 1972 minimum wage keeps not the $64 earned but only $21.33 ($64 less a reduction in welfare payments of $42.67) plus certain work-related expenses. Legislation passed in 1971 requires welfare recipients to accept jobs if offered, regardless of their pref-

---

1. Joel F. Handler, "Federal-State Interests in Welfare Administration" (paper prepared for delivery at the Joint Economic Committee-Institute for Research on Poverty Conference on Income Maintenance Programs, July 1972; processed), p. 8.

2. On this subject, more generally, see Gilbert Y. Steiner, *The State of Welfare* (Brookings Institution, 1971).

erences. But this requirement is unlikely to have constructive results, for reasons to be described below.

Despite the consensus that the present system badly needs repair or reconstruction, the Senate Finance Committee has twice rejected House-passed welfare reform bills, although once it developed largely new proposals of its own. Various committee members have complained about the lack of work incentives in the proposals before it. Chairman Russell B. Long declared that the President's family assistance plan

... finds it necessary to sharply curtail the amount of earnings that a person can retain when he goes to work. Otherwise, the mathematics of the plan makes it [sic] cost prohibitive. The administration-supported formula would reduce the overall family income by $2 for every $3 earned. In many cases, after one considers the increase in social security taxes paid, the loss of medicaid benefits, and especially if the family is enjoying the benefit of subsidized public housing, the family income would be reduced by more than 100 percent of every dollar that a father or mother proceeded to earn.[3]

Senator Long's criticism was telling because it indicted the family assistance plan for reducing work incentives, one of the problems in the existing system that it was designed to solve. His criticism raises another issue, ignored until recently by advocates of welfare reform: the difficulties created by the interaction between cash assistance and subsidization of housing, food, and medical care. Most welfare recipients receive benefits under at least one other program. Virtually all receive health care benefits under the medicaid program; 68 percent receive free food under the commodity distribution program or food subsidies under the food stamp program; 13 percent live in low-rent public housing, and a growing fraction receives assistance under one of the other federal housing programs. To compound the present multibenefit situation, a variety of proposals to offer the poor subsidized day care services is waiting in the political wings, and an income-conditioned college scholarship program became law in 1972. Under all of these programs, the amount of assistance declines, often quite precipitously, as income rises. These implicit taxes add to those in the welfare system and further reduce the net gain to recipients from working.

Senator Long's criticisms of the family assistance plan highlight the impossibility of increasing work incentives through welfare reform alone. All

3. *Welfare Reform: Or Is It?* Address of Hon. Russell B. Long, Chairman, Senate Committee on Finance, and Supporting Material, Committee on Finance, 92 Cong. 1 sess. (1971), p. 5.

programs to help the poor—cash assistance, housing subsidies, medicaid, food stamps, and commodity distribution—must be reformed simultaneously if the poor are to be given genuine economic incentives to maintain or increase work effort. The need for a comprehensive approach arises because income determines both eligibility and the level of benefits under all programs. The prospect of extending assistance to families headed by fully employed men, and by women not covered under present law, accentuates the need for improved incentives in the welfare system.

Chapter 2 describes the present melange of welfare programs. Despite years of controversy and study, few understand these programs and their interactions in detail. Chapter 3 discusses recent efforts to reform welfare, none of which has so far threaded the political maze separating proposals from law. Chapter 4 explores the difficulties in reforming welfare while preserving the incentive to work. It makes clear that "work incentives" may be defined in different ways and that some incentives are easier to preserve than others. Chapter 5 examines a variety of means by which work incentives may be increased, and concludes that none of the commonly advanced proposals to improve incentives, such as the negative income tax, wage subsidies, or demogrants, will work unless it is integrated with major programs of in-kind assistance. Chapter 6 briefly outlines desirable steps toward welfare reform.

CHAPTER TWO

Aid to the Poor

Only in the last decade have programs to assist the poor received much attention. Until the late sixties low-income Americans receiving federal, state, or local assistance were a small minority. Although the officially counted poor numbered 39.8 million in 1960, only 7.1 million received public assistance, roughly 2 million lived in low-rent public housing (the only important program of housing assistance then in operation), and 4.3 million received surplus agricultural commodities. Few households benefited from more than one of these programs. Food stamps, medicaid and medicare, and numerous programs of housing assistance awaited enactment. Not only did the poor belong to the "other America" to which few paid much attention, but the assisted poor formed only a small portion of this obscure colony. That the programs were defective in design was known to a few, but this knowledge was politically irrelevant.

By 1970 all of this had changed. The number of poor had declined to 25.5 million, but their political significance had increased, partly through their own organizational efforts, partly through a blossoming of conscience and concern by others. The number of public assistance beneficiaries almost doubled to 13.8 million, and, at $14.4 billion, payments were nearly four times their earlier amount. Roughly 2.5 million people lived in public housing. Food stamps and surplus agricultural commodities were used by more than 10 million persons. The Housing and Urban Development Act of 1968 pledged the nation to build 6 million federally assisted housing units in the following decade under the numerous housing assistance programs that had come into existence. Together with low-rent public housing

5

already in existence, these units would provide subsidized housing for 25 million to 30 million people. By 1971, medicaid was providing largely free medical care for 18.2 million persons receiving funds under the program of aid to families with dependent children (AFDC) or classed as medically indigent, while medicare subsidized care for 20 million aged Americans; the total cost of these two programs was $10.5 billion.

The simultaneous decline in poverty and the creation of new subsidy programs assured that a growing number of families received benefits under two, three, or more programs, as these data demonstrate:[1]

Program	Percent of recipients of AFDC benefiting from special program
Medicaid	99
Food stamps	53
Food distribution	15
Public housing	13
School lunch	59

The statistics inadequately describe program overlap because they exclude such relevant programs as other forms of public assistance, old age and disability pensions, unemployment insurance, and veterans' pensions and compensation. They do not reveal that the incidence of multiple benefits has climbed steadily and that other income-conditioned programs awaiting consideration, such as subsidized day care, would raise it still more.

The existence of program overlap assures recipients more adequate support than any single program can provide. But overlap creates problems. Each program was designed with little consideration of the others. They pass through different committees in Congress and are administered independently by different executive departments. As a result, the separate criteria for eligibility and for benefit levels are applied in ways that sometimes seem capricious and senseless. A brief description of the history

1. James R. Storey, *Public Income Transfer Programs: The Incidence of Multiple Benefits and the Issues Raised by Their Receipt,* Studies in Public Welfare, Paper 1, Prepared for the Use of the Subcommittee on Fiscal Policy of the Joint Economic Committee, 92 Cong. 2 sess. (1972), Table 8, p. 26.

and operation of the major programs will show how these anomalies arise.[2]

Cash Assistance

Public assistance was born in 1935 along with the social security system. Unlike pensions for the aged, public assistance was a joint state-federal program. In fact, the states have adopted such diverse benefit levels and administrative rules that fifty-one separate public assistance programs are in operation in the states and the District of Columbia. The creators of public assistance did not expect it to grow. Public assistance for the aged was expected to wither as eligibility expanded and benefits increased under social security, but the number of recipients has barely changed in three decades. The number of AFDC recipients was expected to decline modestly as the economy recovered from the depression. Contradicting expectations, however, AFDC grew steadily during the 1950s and more rapidly in the 1960s as it came increasingly to serve mothers who had never married or who were divorced, deserted, or separated, rather than those who had been widowed, as originally anticipated. By 1971 only 14 percent of AFDC families were headed by widows or contained an incapacitated man; 76 percent were headed by women who were divorced, deserted, separated, never married, or otherwise living apart from their children's fathers; and the remaining 10 percent were intact families, many helped under a program for unemployed fathers, first enacted in 1961. Smaller programs for the blind and for the permanently and totally disabled generated little concern until 1968, except over the adequacy of payments; since then, the number of the disabled has increased sharply as drug addicts and alcoholics have been included.

The issue of work incentives has arisen solely with respect to AFDC and only in the past decade. The notion of compelling the aged, blind, disabled, or widowed to work in order to receive public aid does not stir much enthusiasm; these groups are deemed to have legitimate reasons for not working. For women who are not widows, however, the care of children is not so widely deemed a legitimate reason not to work, particularly if the children are of school age (42 percent of all women with children now work). As the proportion of adult AFDC recipients who are not widows

2. For a comprehensive list of programs offering cash or in-kind assistance, see Studies in Public Welfare, Paper 2, *Handbook of Public Income Transfer Programs,* A Staff Study prepared for the use of the Subcommittee on Fiscal Policy of the Joint Economic Committee, 92 Cong. 2 sess. (1972).

has risen and the idea of supplementing the incomes of the working poor has gained attention, the issue of work incentives has become urgent.

The AFDC program serves two related but distinct functions. It establishes an income floor for selected families. This floor varies from state to state (see Table 2-1). It also meets emergency outlays or special expenses

Table 2-1. Aid to Families with Dependent Children: Standard of Need, Maximum and Average Annual Payments, Average Work-related Expenses, and Percentage of Population, Selected States, 1971[a]

State	Annual amount for basic needs		Annual average work-related expense[d]	Annual average payment per 4-person family	Recipients as percentage of state population
	Full standard[b] (1)	Maximum payment[c] (2)	(3)	(4)	(5)
California	$4,560	$2,652	$1,098	$2,508	7.6%
Colorado	2,820	2,820	304	2,510	4.5
Florida	2,676	1,608	260	1,162	4.6
Georgia	2,496	1,596	370	1,375	6.7
Illinois	3,408	3,408	548	2,803	6.1
Indiana	4,356	1,800	480	1,733	3.0
Iowa	3,600	2,916	265	2,537	2.8
Massachusetts	4,188	4,188	591	3,226	4.9
Michigan	3,516	3,516	345	2,981	5.6
Mississippi	2,784	720	203	670	6.9
Missouri	3,900	1,560	713	1,469	4.5
New Jersey	4,164	4,164	886	3,000	5.3
New York	4,032	4,032	936	3,730	6.9
North Carolina	2,208	1,896	536	1,514	3.3
Pennsylvania	3,756	3,756	562	2,993	5.6
Texas	2,868	2,148	198	1,409	3.6
Vermont	3,924	3,924	240[e]	2,983	3.7
Washington	3,636	3,636	648	2,868	4.3

Sources: For col. 1, U.S. Department of Health, Education, and Welfare, Social and Re-habilitation Service, National Center for Social Statistics, "OAA and AFDC: Standards for Basic Needs for Special Types of Assistance Groups, March 1971," NCSS Report D-2 (3/71) (no date), Table 4, col. 1. For col. 2, *ibid.*, col. 5. For col 3, unpublished estimates by the Urban Institute (March 23, 1972). For col. 4, HEW, SRS, NCSS, "Public Assistance Statistics, March 1971," DHEW, NCSS Report A-2 (3/71) (no date), Table 7, col. 6. For Col. 5, "Public Assistance Statistics, December 1971" (March 1972), Table 14, col. 2.

a. As of March 1971, except col. 5, which is for December 1971.

b. The full standard is the amount with which income from all sources is compared to deter-mine whether financial eligibility exists. Use of the full standard (if different from the payment standard) is mandatory only for AFDC applicant families with earned income who have not re-ceived assistance in any one of the four preceding months. The payment standard is the amount from which income available for basic needs is subtracted to determine the amount of assistance to which a family is entitled.

c. The total monthly payment for basic needs made under state law or agency regulations to families with no other income.

d. In addition, all states except Vermont treat income and payroll taxes as work-related expenses.

e. Vermont permits a flat allowance of $20 a month to part-time workers and $40 a month to full-time workers.

of eligible families. Part of the variation in AFDC payments arises because state welfare agencies have established different standards of need, part because not all states pay recipients the full standard. In addition, states enjoy wide discretion in establishing rules that influence the amount families actually receive. They pay recipients for certain work-related expenses, but each defines them differently. Some, but not all, states reimburse recipients for income and payroll taxes, some for other mandatory payroll deductions, some for transportation, child care, union dues, food away from home, tools, or uniforms. Some states require that recipients, who may be ignorant of allowable deductions, apply for reimbursement in order to receive it. As Table 2-1 indicates, the average allowance differs widely across states, but the table does not indicate the substantial variation in actual reimbursements of work expenses within states. In addition, case workers have considerable administrative discretion in determining which expenses to allow, a power they are alleged to use with varying degrees of generosity to adjust payments for peculiar family needs. States also exercise substantial discretion in determining eligibility for payments. As a result of all these elements, the average payment and the proportion of families receiving benefits vary widely from state to state.

Before 1967 most states reduced welfare payments $1 for each $1 of earnings net of work-related expenses. Some states applied this reduction only after earnings reached a certain level. This arrangement seemed calculated to discourage welfare recipients from seeking employment. Under the current system payments are reduced by a maximum of two-thirds of earnings over $360 per year. However, many work-related expenses rise with income, so that the effective rate of reduction of payments, or the implicit tax rate on earnings, may be considerably less.[3] Work-related expenses averaged about 35 percent of earnings in 1971. Since many states

---

3. Some states are reported to compel recipients to quit work if work-related expenses are too great; see Joel F. Handler, "Federal-State Interests in Welfare Administration" (paper prepared for delivery at the Joint Economic Committee-Institute for Research on Poverty Conference on Income Maintenance Programs, University of Wisconsin, July 1972; processed), p. 3. On the other hand, "Some pro-client caseworkers take pride in generating enough expenses so that allowable income [used to reduce welfare payments] falls to zero." W. Joseph Heffernan, Jr., "Variations in Negative Tax Rates in Current Public Assistance Programs: An Example of Administrative Discretion" (University of Wisconsin, Institute for Research on Poverty, 1972; processed), p. 12.

set welfare payments lower than estimated needs, they enjoy further discretion over the rate at which payments should be reduced.[4]

The degree to which additional work incentives could affect the AFDC caseload remains in hot dispute. According to a 1971 survey by the Department of Health, Education, and Welfare (HEW), of 2.3 million AFDC mothers, 644,800 were working, seeking work, receiving training, or awaiting training; 936,800 were needed in the home full time as homemakers; 478,000 were physically or mentally incapacitated or without marketable skills; and the remaining 286,100, or 12 percent, were not seeking work although presumably able to do so.[5] Those mothers who worked earned an average of $223 per month, but the survey does not report how many hours per week employed mothers worked or how hard those out of work sought it. According to these statistics, with existing limited day care services, a maximum of 12 percent of welfare mothers could be led to seek employment. On the other hand, there is little doubt that, faced with the loss of all public support, many who are not now working would seek and find work. One cannot safely predict, however, how much they would earn or what fraction would fail to find jobs, despite their best efforts.

The various provisions to promote work incentives also create inequities. One family may be eligible for public assistance while another, in precisely the same current circumstances, may not be. This anomaly arises because eligibility is established by a family income that falls below the state needs standard—say, $3,600 per year for a family of four—but is lost in a state that pays the full needs standard only if income rises to at least 150 percent of this standard plus $360—about $6,000.[6] Thus, fami-

---

4. Assume, for example, that a state sets need at $400 per month, but pays only $200 per month. Depending on the method used, a welfare recipient who earns $200 exclusive of work-related expenses and the $30 exclusion may face a reduction of welfare payments of anywhere from $133 to nothing. There will be no reduction if the state disregards earnings equal to the difference between need and the maximum state payment; a $133 reduction if the state applies the basic "two-thirds" formula; or something in between if, for example, the state disregards earnings equal to a part of the gap between state payments and need. The net impact of AFDC and other programs is calculated more precisely in Chapter 3.

5. U.S. Department of Health, Education, and Welfare, Social and Rehabilitation Service, National Center for Social Statistics, *Findings of the 1971 AFDC Study*, Pt. 1, *Demographic and Program Characteristics*, DHEW Pubn. (SRS) 72-03.756, NCSS Report AFDC-1 (December 1971), Table 21.

6. The family's benefit equals $3,600 less applicable earnings, which in turn equal two-thirds of actual earnings less $360. Thus only when earnings reach $5,760 would

lies headed by women with earnings between $3,600 and some amount in excess of $6,000 would receive public assistance only if their incomes had been as low as $3,600 and had not subsequently exceeded the eligibility ceiling.

Details such as this abound in the welfare system and differ in each of the fifty-one systems in the United States. Senator Clifford P. Case declared, upon receiving HEW's *Public Assistance Handbook,* "I was appalled to receive a package of regulations weighing almost six pounds, as thick as the Washington, D.C. telephone directory. Leaving the human element aside, this Handbook is the best possible evidence that the present welfare program is a bureaucratic nightmare."[7] Swollen regulations such as these were written in efforts to deal definitively with countless special family situations. In practice, they leave case workers substantial discretion because responsible officials cannot hope to police such complex regulations, even if they wished to do so. In fact, failure to comply with federal regulations is widespread at the state level.[8]

Housing Assistance

Since 1937 the United States has provided subsidized housing for low-income families. The number of such families has always been vastly larger than the number of subsidized housing units. As late as 1970, 7.2 million families had incomes of $4,000 per year or less, but only 695,515 low-rent public housing units were available for occupancy, and only 69 percent were occupied by households with incomes below $4,000. Few subsidized units were available under other federal or state programs.

---

benefits decline to zero. However, states reimburse work-related expenses fully. If work-related expenses totaled only $160, eligibility would not be lost until income exceeded $6,000.

7. *Departments of Labor, and Health, Education, and Welfare, and Related Agencies Appropriations for Fiscal Year 1971,* Hearings before the Subcommittee of the Senate Committee on Appropriations, 91 Cong. 2 sess. (1970), Pt. 4, p. 1791.

8. California persistently defied not only HEW's regulations but also numerous court orders to obey regulations and statutory requirements. See Peter E. Sitkin, "Welfare Law: Narrowing the Gap between Congressional Policy and Local Practice" (paper prepared for delivery at the Joint Economic Committee-Institute for Research on Poverty Conference on Income Maintenance Programs, July 1972; processed). Sitkin also cites the quarterly HEW Compliance Report for October 1, 1971, that lists " 'questions raised on state compliance with federal requirements' for approximately three-fourths of the states" (*ibid.,* p. B).

The Housing and Urban Development Act of 1968 promises to change this picture radically. It introduced new programs of rental and home-ownership assistance and called for the construction or rehabilitation of 6 million federally subsidized housing units in the ensuing decade.

Many of the occupants of federally assisted housing also receive cash assistance. Forty-four percent of nonelderly continuing residents in low-rent public housing were found to be receiving cash assistance during the 1970 annual review of eligibility for continued occupancy. These fractions will probably rise because of recent increases in federal subsidies to local housing authorities on behalf of low-income tenants. The rent supplement program serves approximately one-half million people even poorer than those served by low-rent public housing. Even under the homeownership assistance program, intended for lower-middle-income families, 7 percent of occupants served in early 1971 reported welfare payments as a primary or secondary source of income.[9]

Despite the proliferation of housing assistance programs, many if not most welfare recipients will continue to reside in unsubsidized housing. The principal reason is that most subsidized housing is new and of relatively good quality so that, paradoxically enough, even with federal subsidies it costs more than the genuinely destitute can afford. Most subsidized housing is occupied by families with annual incomes of $4,000 to $8,000. In addition, many welfare recipients live in rural areas or other regions where subsidized housing is scarce.

By residing in federally assisted housing, welfare recipients benefit from large additional subsidies. The annual average benefit under the home-ownership and rental assistance programs is about $1,000. The median rent supplement payment was $972 in 1969; the average benefit in low-rent public housing was $801 in 1966.[10] Housing programs have been strongly criticized for providing large benefits to a small proportion of families eligible on the basis of income while denying it to others.[11] They

9. *1971 Housing and Urban Development Legislation,* Hearings before the Subcommittee on Housing and Urban Affairs of the Senate Committee on Banking, Housing and Urban Affairs, 92 Cong. 1 sess. (1971), pp. 7, 9.

10. The net benefits of public housing to public assistance recipients are often smaller because welfare departments sometimes reduce rent allowances for public housing occupants.

11. See statement of Senator Carl T. Curtis, in *Housing and Urban Development Legislation of 1970,* Hearings before the Subcommittee on Housing and Urban Affairs of the Senate Committee on Banking and Currency, 91 Cong. 2 sess. (1970), Pt. 1, p. 706; see also the questions posed by Senator John G. Tower in *1971 Housing and Urban Development Legislation,* pp. 4–5.

also raise substantially the value of assistance to those welfare families fortunate enough to qualify for housing subsidies.

Occupants of federally assisted housing typically must pay more for their housing as their income, including public assistance, rises. Rent supplements and rental assistance both charge tenants 25 percent of income up to fair market rent. Recipients of homeownership assistance must devote 20 percent of their incomes to mortgage payments. Tenants in low-rent public housing face a wide range of rent policies established independently by local housing authorities. Since 1969, however, housing authorities have been barred from charging tenants more than one-fourth of income in rent; some charge less. In only a few areas are subsidized tenants free from rent increases when their incomes rise.

At first glance the requirement that tenants pay part of increases in income to reduce the federal subsidy seems fair—federal aid declines with need. However, the increase in housing cost to the tenant, like the decline in welfare payments, is a kind of tax, since it diminishes the amount by which an increase in earnings raises disposable income. The occupant of ordinary housing enjoys better housing when an increase in income encourages him to spend more for housing. As his income rises, the occupant of subsidized housing must pay more for the same housing. Low-rent public housing tenants encounter an alternate hazard: A small increase in income can lead to complete loss of benefits, for in some cases they must move out of the projects if their incomes reach a certain level.

Medical Assistance

Under medicaid, the federal government pays at least half, and states the rest, of the cost of medical care for selected groups, provided that the states offer certain basic medical services. These must include inpatient and outpatient hospital services, other laboratory and x-ray services, skilled nursing home services for people 21 or older, home health care for those eligible for the last, physician services, and early and periodic screening, diagnosis, and treatment of persons under 21 for physical or mental defects, as provided in social security regulations. States may place limits on these benefits.

They may, in addition, define eligibility broadly or narrowly and they may offer many medical services in addition to the required minimum.[12] The number eligible for medicaid is determined both by the size of the population receiving cash assistance and by the state's decision on whether to extend eligibility. The states may secure federal support for some or all of the mandatory or optional medical benefits to families in the public assistance categories whose incomes are not more than one-third above the maximum for cash assistance. For example, a state that will not offer cash assistance to a family with income above $3,000 per year may secure federal support for medical benefits offered to families with incomes up to $4,000 per year.

Since there is wide interstate variation in the level of cash assistance and in the number and extent of medical services provided, and since about half of all states provide some medical benefits to persons not receiving cash assistance, the scope of medicaid programs differs widely. Average medical payments to eligible AFDC families in 1970 and 1971 varied from less than $100 per year in Mississippi to nearly $1,000 per year in New York and Illinois (see Table 2-2). Alaska and Arizona provide no medicaid benefits. Public expenditures per state inhabitant for medical care for all low-income families ranged from $66.05 in New York to $4.25 in Mississippi in 1970;[13] the average was $24.30. These statistics, of course, are averages, and like all averages they conceal wide variations in the value of medical care services received by individual families. However, the average medicaid benefits in the states with the largest welfare caseloads—New York, California, Pennsylvania, Illinois, and Michigan—were $970, $876, $610, $908, and $700, respectively.

The medicaid program indisputably has increased access of eligible low-income households to medical care.[14] The program is so seriously flawed, however, that, almost since its enactment, Congress and medical experts have sought to replace or to revise it extensively. The impact of medicaid on work incentives and the capricious grounds on which eligibility is determined have been prominent in discussions of reform.

12. Various states offer some or all of the following: clinic services, prescription drugs, dental services, prosthetic devices, eyeglasses, private-duty nursing, physical therapy, emergency hospital services, family-planning services, skilled nursing home services for patients under 21, optometrist, podiatrist, or chiropractor services, care in mental or tubercular institutions for patients over 65, and institutional services in intermediate-care facilities.

13. Arizona spent $0.95 per inhabitant on medical care for low-income families under programs other than medicaid.

14. See Charles L. Schultze and others, *Setting National Priorities: The 1973 Budget* (Brookings Institution, 1972), pp. 222–26, especially Table 7-4.

Table 2-2. Income Limits for Medicaid Benefits for the Medically Indigent and Average Medicaid Payment per AFDC Family of Four, Selected States, 1971

Dollars

State	Maximum income for initial eligibility for medicaid benefits for four-person medically indigent family (1)	Average medical vendor payment per AFDC four-person family[a] (2)
California	3,600	876
Colorado	b	344
Florida	b	309
Georgia	b	374
Illinois	3,600	908
Indiana	b	547
Iowa	b	692
Massachusetts	4,176	738
Michigan	3,540	700
Mississippi	b	89
Missouri	b	335
New Jersey	b	491
New York	5,000	970
North Carolina	2,800	503
Pennsylvania	4,000	610
Texas	b	640
Vermont	3,828	668
Washington	4,260	524

Sources: For col. 1, HEW, Social and Rehabilitation Service, Assistance Payments Administration, Division of Program Evaluation, "Income Levels for Medically Needy in Title XIX Plans in Operation, as of December 31, 1971" (March 1972; unpublished tabulation). For col. 2, HEW, SRS, Medical Services Administration, Office of Program Planning and Evaluation, "Average Medical Vendor Payments to Families Receiving AFDC Payments," for fiscal years 1971 and 1970 (March 16, 1972; unpublished tabulation).

a. Average of fiscal years 1970 and 1971.

b. State does not have a program in operation for the medically needy.

Eligibility for medicaid is determined on an "on-off" basis in states without a program for the medically indigent. If a family's income is low enough and it meets other eligibility criteria, it receives free medical care. If its income rises $1 above the eligibility threshold, it loses all benefits. Furthermore, in most states the family does not regain eligibility should its income decline by $1, but only if it declines several hundreds or thousands of dollars. For a family with income near the eligibility threshold and with large medical bills, this "notch" can turn a rise in hourly earnings into financial disaster, and it can make a decision to work longer hours a kind of financial suicide.[15] It can deter a mother with dependent children from accepting a job promotion or working one more day per week.

In states with programs for the medically indigent the relationship between income and eligibility is even more complex. In such states families become eligible if income less medical expenses falls below specified levels. This provision requires families to "spend down" to the eligibility level. A family that has just lost eligibility for cash assistance may, depending on the amount of its medical expenses and state of residence, lose all, some, or none of its medicaid benefits.

The work disincentive incorporated in medicaid is unlike that in federal housing assistance. Housing costs rise gradually with income, but the family does not face a sudden and often major drop in benefits when its earnings cross a certain level (except in low-rent public housing). Under medicaid, increases in family income, within the specified limits, do not affect family benefits; but, at a specific income level, all benefits may cease.

Food Assistance

Two federal programs—food stamps and distribution of commodities—provide low-income families with free or subsidized food.

Food Stamps

Food stamps were used by 10.6 million low-income people in March 1971; more than half also received public assistance; but the rest—over 4 million people—were not receiving public assistance. Federal budget outlays for food stamps totaled $1.6 billion in fiscal year 1971 and will reach $2.3 billion in 1973.

Under the food stamp program, low-income families may purchase coupons in various denominations and use them like cash for most food items. The amount of food stamps a family can buy and their cost vary

15. The 20 percent increase in social security benefits caused serious potential hardship by making some aged social security recipients ineligible for the old age assistance they had been receiving, thereby making them ineligible as well for medicaid. See Letters to the Editor, *New York Times,* July 19, 1972. A provision that took care of this problem was subsequently added to H.R. 1.

Table 2-3. Face Value of Food Stamps and Federal Annual Income Limits, by Family Size, 1972

Family size	Face value of food stamps per year	Maximum annual income for eligibility[a]
1	$ 432	$2,136
2	768	2,796
3	1,104	3,684
4	1,344	4,476
5	1,584	5,280
6	1,824	6,084
7	2,064	6,876
8	2,304[b]	7,680[c]

Source: *Federal Register,* Vol. 37 (April 19, 1972).
a. Households in which all members receive public assistance retain eligibility regardless of income.
b. For each person in excess of eight, $192 is added.
c. For each person in excess of eight, $636 is added.

according to family size and income.[16] Federal regulations make four-person families with monthly incomes of more than $373 ineligible for the program (see Table 2-3). States may set lower limits, however, and most have elected to do so, although eight states have set higher limits. Regardless of income, welfare recipients retain eligibility to buy food stamps worth $288 per year more than they cost. This feature worsens the notch effect—the sudden loss of benefits—when eligibility for welfare is lost. Families of two or more with assets greater than $3,000 are ineligible for food stamps (the figure is $1,500 for a one-person household).

The bonus value of food stamps is a subsidy. The stamps lose some attractiveness if they induce the family to spend more for food than it would without the subsidy. Some families allegedly were deterred from buying food stamps because they are sold in some states only at inconvenient centers or because they seem an unduly complex mechanism. Furthermore the program reached only a modest proportion of potentially eligible families for a number of years.[17]

16. The face value varies from $432 per year for a one-person household to $2,304 for an eight-person household. Food stamps are free to all families with incomes below $240 per year, and to three-person or larger families with incomes below $360 per year. Families with higher incomes pay a portion of the face value of the food stamps to obtain them; increased charges take about 30 percent of any increment in income.

17. Steiner, *State of Welfare,* Chap. 6.

Whatever its merits or demerits on other grounds, the food stamp program clearly diminishes the gain a family derives from an increase in earnings. As earnings rise, the face value of food stamps does not increase, but their cost does. For most families the monthly cost of food stamps rises about $3 for every $10 increase in net income—a 30 percent implicit tax. However, the effective rate on earnings is somewhat lower, as taxes and part of earnings are disregarded in the computation.

Commodity Distribution

The older, but less important, program of commodity distribution provides free food to many low-income households in many areas not served by food stamps. Begun in 1935, commodity distribution served 4 million people in thirty-six states in March 1971. In most of these states the food stamp program was the dominant form of food assistance; only five relied exclusively on commodity distribution. The income limits for eligibility for food stamps and commodity distribution are the same in most states.

Although the commodity distribution program provides food free of charge to eligible households, recipients have little or no choice about the kinds of food they receive. In fact, a prominent motive for the program has been to dispose of surplus agricultural commodities. Critics have periodically faulted commodity distribution for providing selections of groceries better designed to clear local warehouses than to offer balanced or palatable meals. The per capita value of commodity distribution benefits has been quite modest compared with that of food stamps.

Since the commodities are free, increased earnings do not penalize an eligible household so long as it remains within the limits of eligibility. As with medicaid, however, a small increase in earnings may deprive a family of access to free food, leaving the family worse off; this threat may induce a worker, in the interest of maintaining his real income, to forgo a wage increase or the opportunity to work more hours.

Other Programs

In mid-1972 President Nixon signed into law a new federal scholarship program for college students. The program provides up to $1,400 per student per year less "expected family contribution." The exact meaning of this term will be set by the Secretary of Health, Education, and Welfare.

If he follows the guidelines for college officials that have been developed by the College Scholarship Service, the scholarship will be reduced by about 23 percent of gross income in excess of a floor graduated with respect to family size.[18] Students from families with two children and income up to $5,875 would receive the full scholarship. Some public assistance families have gross incomes above this amount, particularly in states with high benefits.

The federal government now supports relatively modest child care programs. Both the President and Congress have expressed interest in expanding the federal role, although they have yet to agree on the proper approach. Because day care is costly—approximately $2,000 per year per preschool child—heavy subsidies will be necessary if low- or middle-income families are to make use of it. If the subsidy were to vary with income, yet another program would claim part of increases in earnings and further reduce monetary work incentives.

Both the new program of scholarships for higher education and the potential day care program illustrate the uncoordinated application of the apparently reasonable policy of varying benefits with income. No mention has been made of free school lunches, veterans' pensions, survivors' insurance, and numerous other programs. As the next chapter indicates, the cumulative effect of all these programs can be devastating to work incentives.

18. See College Scholarship Service, *Manual for Financial Aid Officers, 1971 Revision, Part Five: Need Analysis, Sample Case Studies, Tables* (College Entrance Examination Board, 1971), p. B-3.

CHAPTER THREE

Recent Efforts to Reform Public Assistance

In 1969 President Nixon set forth his family assistance plan (FAP) to reform public assistance. As a replacement for aid to families with dependent children (AFDC), the President proposed a basic benefit of $500 per year for each of the first two family members and $300 for each additional member. In addition, the family could earn up to $60 per month with no reduction in payments. For each $2 of additional gross earnings, payments would be cut by $1—a 50 percent tax—and no allowances were to be made for work-related expenses. Under this formula, four-person families would receive some assistance until income exceeded $3,920. All families with the same number of children and the same income would receive the same federal benefit. The federal government also would pay 30 percent of the cost of supplemental payments states might make. In eight states, welfare payments would have been increased even if the states made no supplementary payments. Forty-two states and the District of Columbia would have to make supplementary payments to maintain prevailing AFDC payments standards. States that made supplementary payments could reduce them at the same time federal benefits were cut. In such states, recipients stood to lose at least $2 in cash assistance for every $3 of earnings.

In all states FAP would have aided many previously ineligible families, principally families with low incomes headed by men—the working poor—although states remained free to exclude the working poor from supplementary payments. Under AFDC half of all states disqualified families if both parents were able-bodied and present, regardless of income. In the other half, a few intact families qualified under the unemployed parent program administered within AFDC, but families with a full-time earner were ineligible for federal support regardless of income. FAP would have extended coverage also to many families headed by women in states where AFDC needs standards were lower than the income ceiling for FAP eligibility. In all, it would have raised from 2.4 million to 3.6 million the number of families aided; increased total cash assistance to families with children from $6.8 billion to $7.8 billion in fiscal year 1972; and pushed welfare costs for adult assistance programs, administration, day care, medicaid, and food stamps from $10 billion to $12.4 billion. The net cost of the plan to the federal government would have been $3.8 billion, including $600 million in fiscal relief to states.

A slightly modified version of the President's plan, H.R. 16311, passed the House in 1970 and moved from the south to the north wing of the Capitol; it was referred to the Senate Finance Committee, from which it never emerged. The committee called on the administration to

... work during the next several days to devise an overall plan for welfare reform which would recognize the contributions made by other aid programs such as public housing, food stamps, rent supplements, and so on. It was also the view of the Committee that monetary incentives for able individuals to reduce or quit gainful employment in order to qualify for larger welfare benefits should be ended. Unfortunately, the Family Assistance Plan continued these disincentives to self-help.[1]

While some observers felt that the conservative Finance Committee relished the chance to delay and perhaps to kill a plan to liberalize welfare benefits, the committee supported its allegations with stunning examples. Earning more, some welfare recipients would have less to spend after their welfare payments were reduced, housing subsidies curtailed, and food stamp charges increased.

The administration responded by making three basic changes in its proposal. It promised to send up draft legislation ending medicaid for AFDC families and setting up the family health insurance plan (FHIP), under which families with no income other than the basic federal FAP allotment ($1,600 for a family of four) would receive free health insurance and families with some earnings would pay a health insurance premium. This proposal would have removed the "notch"—the income level at which a

---

1. Press Release, May 1, 1970, reprinted in *H.R. 16311, The Family Assistance Act of 1970*, Revised and Resubmitted to the Committee on Finance by the Administration, 91 Cong. 2 sess. (1970), p. 2.

small increase in earnings could cause a family to lose a large part or all of its medicaid benefits. But it would have constituted yet another subtraction from increased earnings throughout certain income ranges. In addition, HEW proposed administrative changes that would permit families to obtain food stamps more easily and that would remove notches from the payment schedule. A third change removed a drastic inequity in the original proposal under which families headed by a man could have been eligible for both the federal basic payment and state supplementary payments if the man worked no more than 35 hours per week, but only the basic payment if he worked more than 35 hours. The administration decided that no families of this type would be eligible for supplementary benefits.[2] The administration had previously proposed separate legislation establishing a uniform rent formula for all federally assisted housing; tenants would pay in rent 20 percent of the first $3,500 per year of net income and 25 percent of the excess.

The Senate Finance Committee held hearings, but voted 14 to 1 against reporting out the House bill. Liberals, who felt the plan too modest, and conservatives, who felt it extravagant, joined in opposing the House version of the administration bill. Later in the session, the committee rejected a compromise plan by 10 to 6. In the closing days of the Ninety-first Congress the administration tried to revive the family assistance plan on the Senate floor, but the move failed in end-of-session maneuvering.

The administration reintroduced a modified welfare reform plan in 1971. The House Ways and Means Committee held executive sessions and favorably reported a revised bill. The full House passed this bill, H.R. 1, on June 22, 1971.

H.R. 1

H.R. 1 resembled the family assistance plan passed by the House in the preceding year. Like its predecessor, it provided a basic federal payment to families with little or no income and permitted states to supplement that

---

2. This step solved one problem but perpetuated another. Since intact families received only the federal basic payment while broken families were eligible also for state supplements, the incentive for a family to break up could be substantial. In Pennsylvania, for example, an intact family of five with no outside income would receive $1,900, but if the father deserted the family, payment would jump $3,756 (if the state maintained payment levels). Under current law the incentive to break up is even greater, since the intact family typically receives nothing.

benefit. The basic federal benefit was increased, from $1,600 to $2,400 for a family of four. The differences in benefits by family size are as follows:

Family size	H.R. 1, 1971	Family assistance plan, 1970
2	$1,600	$1,000
3	2,000	1,300
4	2,400	1,600
5	2,800	1,900
6	3,100	2,200
7	3,400	2,500
8[3]	3,600	2,800

On the other hand, H.R. 1 would have made recipients of cash assistance ineligible for food stamps, which were worth about $900 per family to a family of four with $1,600 income. Even with this provision, H.R. 1 was at least as generous as the family assistance plan in low-benefit states—that is, those paying less than $1,600 to a family of four. In the forty-two states that currently paid more than $1,600 per year, however, families would have suffered curtailment of benefits unless the state chose to supplement the federal basic benefit enough to bring total cash assistance up to the sum of current welfare plus food stamp benefits. The abolition of food stamps would have removed one of the several implicit taxes eligible families had to pay on increased earnings.

But H.R. 1 contained a new implicit tax. Families would have been required to pay a medicaid deductible equal to one-third of earnings in excess of a basic floor. This floor was to be $720 plus state supplemental cash assistance, which varied from state to state. This implicit tax would have been operative over different income ranges in various states (according to state supplemental cash assistance and the extent of free medical services) and for various families (according to use of medical services).

H.R. 1 provided that the basic federal payment, as well as state supplements, would be cut by 66⅔ percent rather than 50 percent of earnings in excess of $60 per month. However, deduction of reasonable day care expenses was permitted. The tax would be applied to gross earnings instead of earnings net of social security taxes, income taxes, and work-related expenses, as under the current welfare system. Because of its more generous

3. Under FAP, families with more than eight members would have received $2,800 plus $300 for each member beyond eight.

basic federal benefit and despite its increase in the implicit tax rate, the H.R. 1 plan would pay some benefits to four-person families until earnings exceeded $4,320, compared with $3,920 under FAP.

Twenty-nine states pay more than $2,400 to a family of four, however. If those states supplemented the basic federal benefit, families with higher incomes would be eligible for some support. How much higher is unclear, since H.R. 1 permitted states, in computing state supplements, to tax earnings over $4,320 at rates above (or below) 66⅔ percent.

H.R. 1 set up two categories of adults in beneficiary families. The first consisted of adults from intact families and from all broken families with no child under age 3 (age 6 until 1974); normally one adult from each such family would have been required to register for training or for job referral, including public service employment. Unless in school, dependent youths over age 15 also would have had to register. The bill provided a $30 monthly bonus for participants in training programs and day care for children of registrants to enable them to work or undertake training. Payments to families containing an adult or a youth who refused to register or to take suitable employment or training would have been reduced by $800. The second group, principally mothers of children under age 3, could have registered for work or training if they wished, but would have been eligible for benefits even if they did not.

The Senate Finance Committee began hearings on H.R. 1 on July 27, 1971, but President Nixon's new economic policy, announced on August 15, diverted its attention. The President also removed much of the sense of urgency about welfare reform by asking that the effective date be deferred one year from 1973 as stated in H.R. 1. The first session of the Ninety-second Congress ended with no action on the bill.

In the waning days of the session, however, a conference committee, reconciling the House and Senate versions of a bill that embodied some minor amendments to the Social Security Act, incorporated an amendment introduced by Senator Herman E. Talmadge requiring certain AFDC recipients to register for work and training. The Talmadge amendment resembled the corresponding provisions of H.R. 1, then still bottled up in the Senate Finance Committee. It did not require mothers of children under 6 to register, emphasized that the state's work incentive unit was to provide child care services, and tied work and training to the existing work incentive program (WIN), widely scored as ineffective.[4] Both houses of

4. See, for example, Leonard Goodwin, *Do the Poor Want to Work? A Social-Psychological Study of Work Orientations* (Brookings Institution, 1972).

Congress accepted these amendments, and President Nixon enthusiastically signed them into law, declaring, "No task, no labor, no work is without dignity or meaning that enables an individual to feed and clothe and shelter himself, and provide for his family. We are a nation that pays tribute to the workingman and rightly scorns the free-loader who voluntarily opts to be a ward of the state."[5]

How H.R. 1 would have fared if the new economic policy had been announced at a different time will never be known. Congress clearly was in a mood to support tighter work and training requirements, but equally clearly was not swept by a passion to raise cash assistance and extend it to millions of families. H.R. 1 might never have emerged from committee even had the President's new economic policy not shouldered it aside. The chairman of the Finance Committee, Senator Russell B. Long, had declared skepticism about the plan and intimated that he did not think it a genuine reform. In any case, committee members who disagreed over whether AFDC paid too little or too much to the poor united in dislike of H.R. 1 and killed the version of welfare reform espoused by the administration and passed by the House.

The Long Plan

Under Senator Long's direction, the Senate Finance Committee drafted a substantially different plan to supplement low incomes. Like H.R. 1, the Long plan distinguished two categories of poor families.[6] One group, principally families headed by mothers of children under age 6, would have been eligible for an amended form of AFDC. In connection with this group, block grants would have replaced federal matching grants; and federally mandated rules would have substantially reduced state administrative discretion. States would have been free to raise or lower welfare payments but not below $2,400 for a four-person family; states that paid less than $2,400 would have lost federal support if they cut allotments, but were not

5. *Weekly Compilation of Presidential Documents,* Vol. 8, No. 1 (January 3, 1972), p. 7.

6. All references to the "Long plan" are based on *Social Security and Welfare Reform,* Summary of the Principal Provisions of H.R. 1 as Determined by the Committee on Finance, 92 Cong. 2 sess. (1972), pp. 53–116. Although the Finance Committee retained the House bill number, the Senate version is referred to here as the Long plan to avoid confusion.

obliged to increase them. Although their discretion was restricted, states would have continued to administer payments.

The major innovation of the Long plan was its proposed treatment of families not eligible for the revised AFDC, principally those headed by an able-bodied man or a mother whose children were over the age of 6. This group was to receive a wage subsidy or guaranteed employment. Workers employed in the private sector at less than $2.00 per hour but at least $1.50 would have received two subsidies, one equal to three-fourths of the difference between their actual income and their earnings if they were paid $2.00 per hour, the other equal to 10 percent of gross private earnings. The wage subsidy would not have applied to jobs paying less than $1.50 per hour, and neither subsidy would have applied to earnings received for more than 40 hours of work per week. The 10 percent bonus would have been phased out $1 for every $4 of earnings over $4,000 per year and hence would have vanished when earnings reached $5,600. The maximum annual subsidy, $1,050, would have been paid to workers employed full time at $1.50 per hour, who earned $3,000 per year. Workers employed year-round at the minimum wage of $2.00 per hour would have received a $400 bonus. Those unable to find private employment or employed at less than $1.50 per hour would have been guaranteed jobs by a newly created Work Administration for 32 hours per week at $1.50 per hour, yielding annual earnings of $2,400. Those eligible adults who refused to work would have received no assistance, although AFDC payments might have been made to third parties on behalf of their dependents. Families participating in the employment program would have been barred from buying food stamps. Families eligible for medicaid who earned more than $2,400 would have had the option of retaining benefits, but they would have been required to pay a premium equal to 20 percent of earnings over $2,400 for the privilege.

The Long plan placed strict requirements on states that might have wished to add to the federal subsidy. In computing supplementary benefits, states would have had to assume that families earned at least $2,400 per year and to disregard all earnings up to $4,500 per year. The former provision, in effect, reduced state supplements; the latter denied the state the right to reduce benefits until earnings exceeded the stipulated amount.

The wage subsidy program made no allowance for family size. Although the committee considered an ancillary allowance for large families, it did not report it out. As a result, families would have faced an incentive to dissolve whenever AFDC benefits exceeded $2,400, the most that the

Work Administration would assure. Families that remained eligible for AFDC would have been discouraged from accepting part-time work. They would have been allowed to keep only the first $20 of earnings per month or compelled to switch to the guaranteed job program, in which the wage subsidy might have been considerably smaller.[7]

The Long plan injected an important new element into discussions of welfare reform. Not only did it distinguish two groups among the poor—on the basis of the sex of their heads and the ages of their children—and make one subject to a work test; but also it established two distinct benefit schedules. One schedule provided relatively generous assistance to families with no outside income but afforded virtually no incentive to work. The other provided no assistance to such families but incorporated positive work incentives for the lowest wage workers.

The full Senate rejected the Long plan and declined to revive the welfare reform provisions of H.R. 1 passed by the House of Representatives. After three years of debate over ways to reform a welfare system widely regarded as a mess, the final decision of the Congress left AFDC essentially unchanged.

Demogrants

At roughly the same time that the Long plan emerged from committee, a quite different approach gained widespread attention through the primary campaign for the Democratic presidential nomination. Senator George McGovern announced his support in principle of "demogrants," a set of payments made to all citizens regardless of income. The high cost of substantial demogrants made tax increases or tax reform, or both, mandatory. As an example, Senator McGovern suggested a $1,000 average per capita demogrant financed by a broad income tax levied at the rate of 33⅓ percent. Critics soon discovered that the combined tax system and demogrants would yield much less revenue than the current income tax, even if savings from the termination of welfare payments were added.

The demogrant principle may be examined independently of Senator

7. For other criticisms in a generally sympathetic review of the Long plan, see Robert H. Haveman, "Work-Conditioned Income Supplementation: An Analysis of the Long Bill and A Proposal" (paper prepared for delivery at the Joint Economic Committee-Institute for Research on Poverty Conference on Income Maintenance Programs, University of Wisconsin, July 1972; processed).

McGovern's proposal. It differs from the family assistance plan, H.R. 1, and the Long plan in important respects. It is paid not only to families with children but to childless couples and single persons. It may or may not be combined with a work requirement. Since advocates customarily have regarded demogrants as a perquisite of citizenship or as an element of the tax system, however, they have not emphasized work requirements.

The chief purpose of demogrants is to establish a basic income floor in such a way that all citizens feel that they participate in the system and low-income recipients are relieved of stigma. A sufficiently generous demogrant, therefore, could meet the income support function of the welfare system. It could not, however, fulfill the second function of the welfare system—meeting emergency needs and special requirements of certain families; consequently, some form of special aid would remain necessary, although on a much reduced scale.

Advocates of a combination of demogrants and amended income taxation emphasize the simplicity and comprehensibility of the proposed arrangements relative to the complexities housed within the Internal Revenue Code and welfare systems. Simplicity, however, carries a price. The special provisions of both the welfare system and the tax code mean more income for specific groups. Some special tax provisions are defended only by their beneficiaries; others command widespread support. In any case, the replacement of a complex arrangement by a simple system that yields approximately the same amount of revenue, particularly one intended to increase assistance to the poor, is bound to raise taxes for many people. Some of these increases will be the necessary and intended consequence of tax reform; others will be unintentional. For example, a demogrant that provided $1,200 for each adult and $600 per child and taxed the first $15,000 of income at 33⅓ percent would guarantee a couple with two children and no income $3,600, more than the current AFDC payment in all but a few states. If a four-member family had income of $15,000, it would pay $1,400, compared with $1,820 under the current system. But single people with a $15,000 income would face a tax increase from $2,702 under current law to $3,800. Whether or not in some ideal world the single person should pay more tax while four-person families should pay less, such redistributions of tax burdens as this are not widely considered to be important, and they are likely to increase opposition to demogrants. Yet provisions that protect "innocent" or "deserving" groups inevitably would reintroduce complexity. The twin objectives—simplification and redistribution to the poor at the expense primarily of those who enjoy widely acknowledged loopholes in the tax system—are inconsistent.

Other Programs

In the period since 1969, while debates over cash assistance have proceeded, completely independent efforts to reform housing assistance and medicaid have been under way. In 1970 the Nixon administration proposed to consolidate the scores of federal housing programs. The bill would have replaced all programs to assist tenants—rental assistance, rent supplements, low-rent public housing, and several smaller subsidized programs—with one program. Tenants would have been required to pay one-fifth of the first $3,500 of income and one-fourth of the excess in rent; the federal government would have paid the rest of fair market rents, up to a specified maximum. Also, programs to subsidize home purchases, principally the homeownership assistance program enacted in 1968, were to have been consolidated. Homeowners would have been required to devote 20 percent of income to mortgage payments; the federal government would have paid the rest, again subject to limits. A slightly revised version, requiring tenants in assisted housing to pay one-fourth of income in rent, passed the Senate in March 1972, but was killed by the House in September.

Discontent over many aspects of the medicaid program led the Nixon administration to propose the family health insurance plan as an alternative. The revision of FAP, submitted by the administration to the Senate Finance Committee in June 1970, promised new health proposals as part of the 1972 budget. The budget retained services comparable to medicaid for adult recipients of public assistance. For families with children, FHIP would have provided a range of medical services worth about $680 per year to a family of four. The services would have been free for families of four within incomes below $3,000; premiums, deductibles, and coinsurance, amounting to an implicit tax of about 15 percent, would have been imposed on families with incomes of $3,000 to $5,000. A family of four would have been ineligible if its income exceeded $5,000. Congress has taken no action on FHIP.

The House Ways and Means Committee included a revision of medicaid in H.R. 1. It called for a medicaid deductible equal to one-third of income over a minimum that varies from state to state. But this deductible died with welfare reform in the Senate. The Long plan would have charged families a premium equal to 20 percent of income over $2,400 per year for medicaid. The fate of these proposals suggests that reform of medicaid has become part of the larger questions of how to assure all families adequate medical care and how to improve efficiency in the delivery of medical services. Major reform in medicaid may have to await decisions on these broader issues.

In summary, the past four years have witnessed a remarkable number of proposals for changes in cash, housing, health, and food assistance, but remarkably little action. The reason for inaction is not the absence of concern about the present system, but rather the intense divisiveness of these programs. While differences in philosophy and values go far in explaining these controversies, technical issues, centering on the preservation of work incentives, are prominent. The next chapter examines the work incentive problem that welfare reform must solve.

CHAPTER FOUR

Obstacles to Reform

Welfare policy has customarily distinguished several categories among the poor—the aged; the seriously disabled or ill; and among those neither old nor sick, families with children headed by men, families with children headed by women, childless couples, single people. Separate forms of assistance support the aged and the disabled and blind. These groups and the programs serving them are ignored in all that follows since the problem of work incentives does not apply to them.

Cash assistance and medicaid are available to families headed by women, but with the minor exception of the unemployed parent program under aid to families with dependent children (AFDC) and some state-financed cash assistance, neither is available to families headed by men or to single people. Food stamps, public housing, and other forms of housing assistance are available to families with male heads as well. The housing programs serve families with higher income than those served by the other programs, but the number of subsidized units is far smaller than the number of eligible households. Single, nonelderly people receive little assistance.

The fifty-one public assistance systems and the programs to improve the housing, health care, and diets of the poor have all been criticized for numerous particular shortcomings, some of which have been presented in earlier chapters. A serious joint shortcoming of the programs is that they interact to form a system that is inequitable and discourages work.

First, each program provides rather substantial benefits, but only to a fraction of the families eligible on the basis of income. AFDC covers few families headed by an unemployed man, none headed by a fully employed man, and no childless couples or single persons. Food stamps go unused by millions of eligible families. Medicaid is unavailable in two states, and elsewhere coverage and the number of services vary widely. Housing assistance directly reaches only a small fraction of low-income families because many cannot afford assisted housing, too few units are available to house all who are eligible, and assisted housing is wholly lacking in many rural areas where the poor are concentrated.

Second, states set income limits for eligibility at widely different levels in all except the housing programs. Within such limits some states are far stricter than others in determining eligibility. The reasons for such variations are numerous and debatable—incomes and political attitudes differ across states, for example—but the consequences are clear and inequitable: Whether a family receives assistance may depend on where it lives.

The third difficulty, related to the second, is that benefit levels vary greatly from state to state for families in the same circumstances. Not only do standards of need and of payments differ, but so also do state practices in determining work-related expenses and in offsetting earnings against assistance payments. In addition, the requirement that a family's income in the past must have fallen below a particular level for it to become eligible for AFDC means that one family may receive benefits while another with the identical current income may not. Food stamp benefits vary because they are tied to cash income, which in turn depends on welfare payments. Housing benefits, except in low-rent public housing, are uniform because they are set by federal regulations. Public housing benefits vary because local housing authorities have wide discretion in setting rents. As a result of all these provisions, some families are "leap-frogged" over others. A family with little or no earnings may end up with more disposable income than one earning thousands of dollars more.

The problem of work disincentives arises because of the high implicit tax rate within AFDC, and is aggravated by the implicit taxes in other forms of assistance. Nearly all AFDC recipients are also eligible to receive other support through medicaid, and many through commodity distribution or food stamps; and an increasing proportion is eligible for federal housing assistance.

Figures 4-1 and 4-2 show the full effect of income taxes, reductions in AFDC payments, increased charges for food stamps and assisted housing, and the value of lost medicaid eligibility for a family of four in a hypothetical state with an AFDC payment standard and actual payments

Figure 4-1. Tax Rates for a Family of Four under Aid for Families with Dependent Children Alone and in Combination with In-kind Benefits, by Earnings Level, 1972

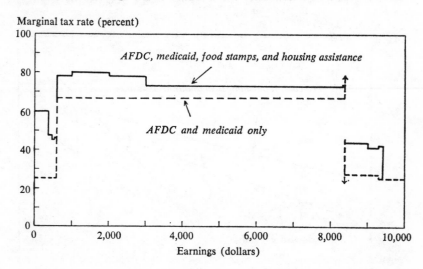

Marginal tax rate (percent)

AFDC, medicaid, food stamps, and housing assistance

AFDC and medicaid only

Earnings (dollars)

Sources: Derived using the following assumptions and conditions: Recipients of AFDC and medicaid only pay social security taxes at 5 percent of earnings, federal personal income taxes at 1972 statutory rates, state income taxes at 2 percent of earnings above $5,000 and below $7,000 and 4 percent on earnings above $7,000; they incur work-related expenses equal to one-fifth of the first $3,000 in earnings, for which AFDC provides full reimbursement. AFDC is worth $3,600 per year for a family with no earnings; medicaid benefits are worth $1,000 to a family of four.

Recipients of the full range of assistance receive, in addition to AFDC and medicaid, food stamps with a face value of $1,344 and housing assistance equal to

$$1,800 - 0.25[0.9(E{-}T) + CA],$$

where E denotes earnings; T, taxes; and CA, cash assistance.

of $3,600 per year and a medicaid plan worth $1,000 per year. The marginal tax rate is the ratio of the change in after-tax resources—the sum of earnings less taxes, cash assistance, and the face value of in-kind benefits—to the change in before-tax earnings. Figure 4-1 shows the tax rates and Figure 4-2 the disposable cash resources for two families, both receiving AFDC and medicaid, and one receiving in addition food stamps and housing assistance. Both figures presume that the state exactly reimburses the household for all additional expenses associated with work.

Figures 4-1 and 4-2 reveal two striking facts. First, the marginal tax rates are high and capricious. On all earnings from $576 to $8,390 per year, the family eligible solely for AFDC and medicaid faces a tax rate of 67 percent. Eligibility for food stamps and housing assistance raises the tax rate as high as 80 percent, and brings it to 73 percent over the income

Figure 4-2. Value of Disposable Cash Resources Plus In-kind Benefits for Family of Four under Aid for Families with Dependent Children, for Two Combinations of Benefits, by Earnings Level, 1972

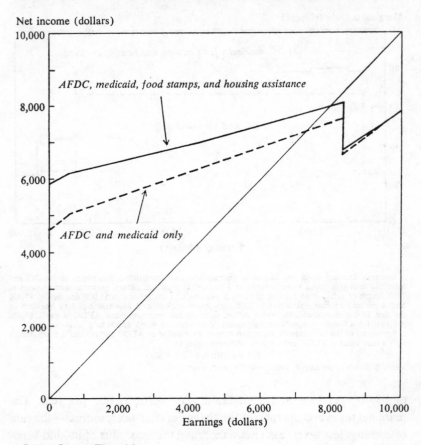

Net income (dollars)

AFDC, medicaid, food stamps, and housing assistance

AFDC and medicaid only

Earnings (dollars)

Source: Same as Figure 4-1.

range from $4,000 to $8,300. When earnings reach $8,390, the family is removed from the welfare rolls and at that instant loses $1,000 medicaid benefits and, if eligible, a $288 food stamp bonus.

Figures 4-1 and 4-2 describe how the system is supposed to work. In actual operation, its impact on work incentives is less severe, because the state may "reimburse" client families for certain expenses they would have had in any case (such as lunch) and because case workers may stretch the definition of these expenses. Recent research has revealed that the effective tax rates confronting welfare recipients, even those receiving medicaid, food stamps, and housing assistance, are below 50 percent for AFDC families with modest earnings.[1]

The second striking fact is that the family benefiting from the full range of assistance—cash, medical, food, and housing—receives a rather substantial basic guarantee, $5,860. Cash assistance alone is $3,600, medicaid is worth $1,000, food and housing add $1,260 more. Although most families do not receive all four kinds of benefits, an increasing number are becoming multiple beneficiaries.

In concrete terms, these figures indicate that a mother of three, lucky enough to live in one of the relatively generous states underlying the data and to receive benefits under all four programs, can count on a basic guarantee of $5,860. If she can earn $2,000 working part time, her net spendable income will rise $556. But out of the next $5,000 she might earn, her income would rise only $1,307. In fact, her net income would be higher if she earned $4,000 than if she earned $8,400, because of the loss of medicaid and food stamps.

The Importance of the Work Incentive Question

Is it important to increase work incentives? If so, how can it be done?

Work incentives are an important issue even under the current system. Forty-two percent of all mothers with children under the age of 18 were in the labor force in 1970; 32 percent of mothers of children under the age of 6 and 52 percent of mothers with no child under the age of 6 were in the labor force.[2] Although the fraction of mothers who might work probably would be smaller among AFDC recipients than among the general population, some of the 936,800 AFDC mothers thought to be needed at home might seek employment if AFDC were unavailable or if they could retain

---

1. Leonard Hausman finds that a family of four sustains a tax rate below 50 percent in Chicago, Illinois, if earnings are below $4,300; in St. Louis, Missouri, if earnings are below $6,563; and in Wilmington, Delaware, if earnings are below $3,200. At higher earnings, tax rates typically do not exceed 67 percent. See Leonard J. Hausman, "Cumulative Tax Rates and the Process of Welfare Reform" (paper prepared for delivery at the Joint Economic Committee-Institute for Research on Poverty Conference on Income Maintenance Programs, University of Wisconsin, July 1972; processed), Tables 1, 2, 3.

2. Charles L. Schultze and others, *Setting National Priorities: The 1973 Budget* (Brookings Institution, 1972), p. 256.

more of their earnings than that program allows. Furthermore, millions of low-income families not on welfare face high marginal tax rates as a price of food stamps, federal housing assistance, and medicaid; they pay about 30 percent of increases in income for food stamps and up to 25 percent for housing, and in some states they may suffer loss of health benefits worth an average of $1,000 per year—and far more for particular families—if their earnings pass a stipulated level. The problem of work disincentives is not confined to AFDC recipients, although they face the highest marginal tax rates.

Most welfare reform proposals would broaden the coverage of income support. The H.R. 1 plan and the wage subsidy proposal of Senator Long would have extended assistance to male-headed families with children. The demogrant proposal would benefit all families including childless couples and single people. The work incentive question, therefore, is of even greater importance under proposed welfare reforms.

The economic effect of income support is still subject to considerable uncertainty. Using data collected for other purposes, several economists have tried to determine how sensitive low-income families are to high tax rates.[3] Their studies agree that a large transfer of cash causes some to work less hard, either by working fewer hours or by withdrawing from the labor force altogether, and that higher tax rates also tend to cause reduced work effort. They also suggest that groups marginally attached to the labor force, such as teenagers and women, are more sensitive to both of these influences than are prime-age men, particularly men who are parents of school-age children.

Although these studies agree on the qualitative effects of income maintenance plans, they disagree on their size. At one extreme, Christensen

3. See, for example, Harold Watts and Glen Cain, *Income Maintenance and Labor Supply: Econometric Studies* (Markham Press, forthcoming), for a review of currently available evidence. See also Sandra S. Christensen, "Income Maintenance and the Labor Supply" (Ph.D. thesis, University of Wisconsin, 1972); Christopher Green and Alfred Tella, "Effect of Nonemployment Income and Wage Rates on the Work Incentives of the Poor," *Review of Economics and Statistics,* Vol. 51 (November 1969), pp. 399–408; Robert E. Hall, "Wages, Income and Hours of Work in the U.S. Labor Force," Working Paper 62 (Massachusetts Institute of Technology, August 1970; processed); Michael J. Boskin, "Income Maintenance Policy, Labor Supply and Income Redistribution," Research Memorandum 111 (Stanford University, Research Center in Economic Growth, May 1971; processed); Edward D. Kalachek and Fredric Q. Raines, "Labor Supply of Lower Income Workers," in The President's Commission on Income Maintenance Programs, *Technical Studies* (1970), pp. 159–85.

finds that a guarantee of $2,400 to a family of four, with a 33 percent tax rate, would lead to an aggregate reduction in hours worked by young recipients of 33 to 39 percent and by older recipients of 12 to 16 percent.[4] Kalachek and Raines predict a 46 percent decline in family work effort (37 percent by male members) from an income maintenance plan with a $2,400 guarantee and a 50 percent tax rate.[5] At the other extreme, David Greenberg and Marvin Kosters predict only a 15 percent reduction in labor supply by male family members from such a plan; Irwin Garfinkel predicts that an even more generous plan, providing a $3,000 guarantee and a 50 percent tax rate, would cause able-bodied husbands to reduce their labor supply by 3 percent or less.[6]

Research now under way on the behavior of low-income families headed by prime-age males who received income support at various levels and subject to various tax rates may help to narrow the range of uncertainty.[7] Other experiments involving transfers to rural and other types of families are also in progress. As with all social experiments, the limited duration of payments and the inevitable importance of special local circumstances may cast doubt on the generalizations these trials suggest.

To complicate matters still further, one cannot be sure what tax rate welfare recipients now think they face, or what tax rate they and other families would perceive in some other system. The behavior of recipients will depend on the world as they perceive it, not necessarily as it is. Since the existing system is exceedingly complex and full of uncertainty and since most alternative plans are far from simple, this distinction is quite important. It suggests that the form, as well as the content, of any alternative to the current welfare system is significant. A system with high, but

4. See Christensen, "Income Maintenance and the Labor Supply," pp. 144–45.
5. Reported by Watts and Cain in the manuscript for their forthcoming book cited in note 3 above.
6. *Ibid.*
7. For a description of this research, see Harold W. Watts, "The Graduated Work Incentive Experiments: Current Progress," in American Economic Association, *Papers and Proceedings of the Eighty-third Annual Meeting, 1970* (*American Economic Review,* Vol. 61, May 1971), pp. 15–21; Mordecai Kurz and Robert G. Spiegelman, "The Seattle Experiment: The Combined Effect of Income Maintenance and Manpower Investments," *ibid.,* pp. 22–29; Terence F. Kelley and Leslie Singer, "The Gary Income Maintenance Experiment: Plans and Progress," *ibid.,* pp. 30–38; James N. Morgan, "Discussion," *ibid.,* pp. 39–42, reprinted by Institute for Research on Poverty as *Current Status of Income Maintenance Experiments,* Reprint 73 (University of Wisconsin, 1971).

obscure, marginal tax rates may deter work less than a system with lower, but clearly visible, tax rates.

Another issue concerns the way in which potential workers respond to different income support programs. The crucial decision for a potential worker in most situations is whether or not to work. Once that decision is made, he may have little choice about how many hours to work. Although certain low-status occupations lend themselves to flexible work weeks—domestic service or casual construction labor, for example—regular jobs typically demand a full workweek and permit little absenteeism. This fact may help explain why the work effort of prime-age males appears to respond less than that of women and the young to variations in taxes.

That the work incentive question is politically vital is beyond dispute, as remarks by congressmen and senators other than Senator Russell B. Long (see Chapter 3) continually attest.[8] It is important, therefore, to reduce apparent as well as real work disincentives to a minimum.

Welfare Reform Proposals and the Problem of Work Incentives

H.R. 1

The stated goals of the family assistance plan and of H.R. 1 included the improvement of work incentives. Senator Long claimed that both failed in this regard. Figures 4-3 and 4-4 indicate that he was right.[9] They graph the marginal tax rates and benefits for a family of four that receives (a) cash assistance only and (b) cash assistance, medicaid, and housing assistance. The family is assumed to be eligible for the $2,400 federal guarantee and a $1,200 state supplement under H.R. 1, the same total cash benefit as in Figure 4-1.

Figures 4-3 and 4-4 support two conclusions. First, H.R. 1 would have sharply increased the tax rate on earnings because it denied reimbursement for work-related expenses. In addition, families would have been required to pay one-third of earnings over a certain minimum toward medical expenses. Although these figures are drawn for a state that would

8. See, for example, *Congressional Quarterly Almanac*, 1970 (CQ, 1971), pp. 1034—40.

9. For a similar, but more detailed, criticism of H.R. 1, tracing its congressional history, see Jodie T. Allen, "A Funny Thing Happened on the Way to Welfare Reform" (Urban Institute, January 1972).

Figure 4-3. Tax Rates for a Family of Four under H.R. 1 Alone and in Combination with In-Kind Benefits, by Earnings Level

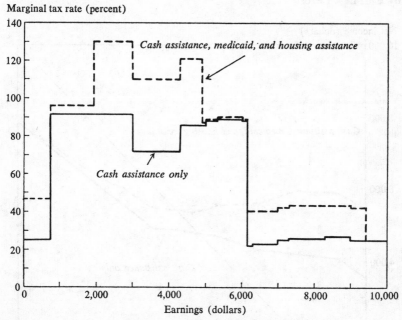

Marginal tax rate (percent)

Cash assistance, medicaid, and housing assistance

Cash assistance only

Earnings (dollars)

Sources: Derived using the following assumptions: Under H.R. 1, a family of four receives a $2,400 federal guarantee and a $1,200 state supplement. The state tax rate, like that imposed by the federal government, is 66⅔ percent. Taxes and work-related expenses are the same as in Figures 4-1 and 4-2. Medical benefits are worth $1,000 and actual medical expenses are $1,000. The 33⅓ percent deductible applies to earnings between $1,920 and $4,920 per year. Housing assistance is computed as in Figures 4-1 and 4-2.

have added a $1,200 supplement to the federal guarantee, this conclusion holds regardless of state policy on supplementation. H.R. 1 would have raised the tax rate for workers earning between $720 and $6,120 per year, a range that includes virtually all of the working poor. Tax rates around 90 percent would prevail in much of this range, compared with 66⅔ percent under the present system for workers receiving cash assistance only. The bill would have curtailed benefits for all such four-person families earning less than about $8,400 per year. The recipient of cash assistance, medicaid, and housing assistance would face super-confiscatory tax rates as high as 130 percent. Rates would exceed 100 percent for workers earning between $1,920 and $4,920,[10] and would not fall much below 90 per-

10. Earnings from full-time, year-round employment at the minimum wage would equal $3,200.

Figure 4-4. Disposable Cash Resources for a Family of Four under H.R. 1 Alone and in Combination with In-kind Benefits, by Earnings Level

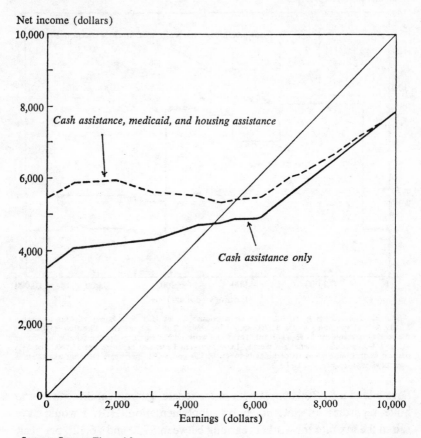

Sources: Same as Figure 4-3.

cent until earnings exceeded $6,120 per year. A worker who earned $6,864 would not have any more net income than a worker earning $1,920.

Second, H.R. 1 would have reduced benefits in states that now pay at least $2,400 to a family of four with no income. This situation would have arisen because H.R. 1 made recipients ineligible for food stamps and because the tax rate applied to gross rather than net earnings. The reduction in benefits could have approached $2,000 a year.

All of these comparisons ignore the fact that H.R. 1 would have increased cash assistance in many states and extended assistance to many currently ineligible families, particularly those headed by men. Furthermore, they ignore the removal or reduction under H.R. 1 of many notches—the levels at which a small increase in income or work now precipitates a large loss of benefits. They do indicate that AFDC imposes formidable tax rates on recipients and that the work disincentives contained in H.R. 1 as passed by the House of Representatives were even worse. They were worse because they would have burdened current welfare recipients with increased tax rates, even in excess of 100 percent, and because they would have applied to many more workers.

The Long Plan

Figures 4-5 and 4-6 demonstrate how families with an employable adult would have fared under the Long plan. The Long plan would have modified AFDC in several important ways for families without an employable adult,[11] but these changes are not shown in these charts.

The Long plan drastically reduced assistance to families containing an employable adult. The reduction was particularly striking if such an adult did not work; no allowance was to be paid unless the state chose to provide some assistance. As earnings rose, the wage and earnings subsidy contained in the Long plan also would have increased. But total federal assistance would have remained smaller than under AFDC or H.R. 1 for a family of four at all earnings levels, though the family might have received more if the state chose to supplement the federal bonus. Because the Long plan bonus did not vary with family size, it might have exceeded current benefits or those proposed in H.R. 1 for two- or three-person families at certain earnings levels; it would have fallen even further below those benefits for families containing more than four persons.

The Long plan substantially reduced the tax rate confronting low-wage workers. In fact, for workers at the very lowest wage levels (three-quarters of the minimum wage), it provided genuinely negative tax rates (that is, subsidies). Even after allowance for the added costs of working (excluding day care) and social security taxes, the Long plan increased the net wage above the nominal wage earned by such workers. However, changes in earnings arising from increases in hourly wage rates between

11. In contrast with H.R. 1, the Long plan did not regard mothers of children 3 to 6 as employable.

Figure 4-5. Tax Rates for a Family of Four under the Long Plan Alone and in Combination with In-Kind Benefits, by Earnings Level

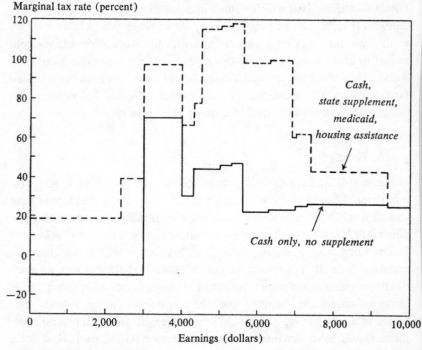

Marginal tax rate (percent)

Cash, state supplement, medicaid, housing assistance

Cash only, no supplement

Earnings (dollars)

Sources: Derived using the following assumptions: The worker is employed at $1.50 per hour for the first $3,000 of annual earnings and thereafter at a gradually increasing rate that reaches $5.00 per hour at $10,000 annual earnings. In Case A the worker receives Long plan benefits only. In Case B he receives Long plan benefits plus a $1,200 state supplement phased out at the rate of $1 for each $2 of earnings over $4,500, medicaid benefits worth $1,000 for which he pays a premium equal to one-fifth of earnings between $2,400 and $7,400, and housing assistance computed as in Figures 4-1 and 4-2.

three-quarters of the minimum wage and the minimum wage were to be taxed at the net rate of 70 percent. Workers earning more than $2.00 per hour were to face only modest taxes and to receive a bonus of up to $400 apart from any supplement paid by the states. The tax rate above $4,500 depended on whether the state supplemented federal support and on the way in which the state phased out such supplementation; the effective rate could have been quite high.

Operating in isolation, the Long plan would have created greater work incentives than H.R. 1 or the current AFDC system. Both the wage subsidy and the denial of benefits to families deemed capable of work would have worked to strengthen work incentives.

Figure 4-6. Disposable Cash Resources for a Family of Four under the Long Plan Alone and in Combination with In-kind Benefits, by Earnings Level

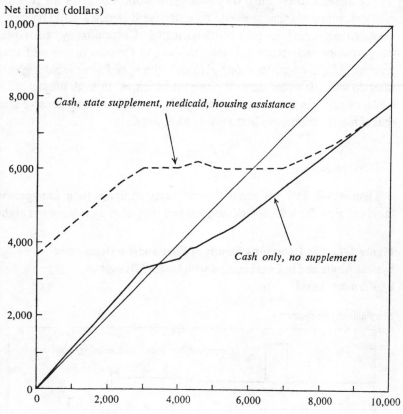

Sources: Same as Figure 4-5.

The Long plan would not have operated in isolation, however, but in combination with other programs. When account is taken of the charge for medicaid of 20 percent of gross earnings over $2,400 and added charges for assisted housing, both the level of assistance and the tax imposed on workers rose sharply under the Long plan. Benefits reached $3,730 (including a $1,200 state supplement). Tax rates would have remained somewhat below those called for in H.R. 1, but still would have exceeded 100 percent at points and averaged just under 100 percent on increments to earnings between $3,000 and $6,900 per year. This tax schedule would have applied to families headed by men, and families headed by women with no child under age 6. The tax schedule faced by female-headed families with small children would have been confiscatory.

The attempt to establish widely different work incentives for two distinct categories of families would be attractive if families could be neatly classified according to their work potential. Unfortunately, such neat categorization is impossible. Many mothers in families that would have received AFDC under the Long plan and who would have faced high tax rates do work or would do so if given the incentive. Indeed, the statistical evidence suggests that the labor supply of women is more responsive than that of men to differences in tax rates on earnings.

Demogrants

Figures 4-7 and 4-8 show the tax rates applying to a four-person family eligible for a $3,600 demogrant and subject to an income tax at the

Figure 4-7. Tax Rates for a Family of Four under a Demogrant System Alone and in Combination with In-kind Benefits, by Earnings Level

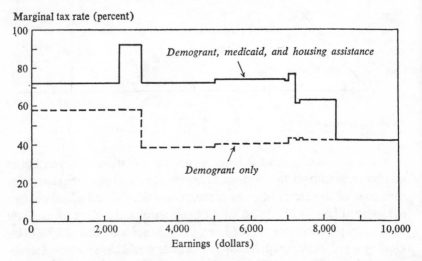

Sources: Derived using the following assumptions: Demogrants are $3,600 per year for a family of four. The family pays social security and state income taxes and incurs unreimbursed work-related expenses at the same level as in Figures 4-1 and 4-2. Federal income taxes are set equal to 33⅓ percent of earnings without deductions or exemptions. Medicaid is treated as under the Long plan. Housing assistance is computed as in Figures 4-1 and 4-2.

Figure 4-8. Disposable Cash Resources for a Family of Four under a Demogrant System Alone and in Combination with In-kind Benefits, by Earnings Level

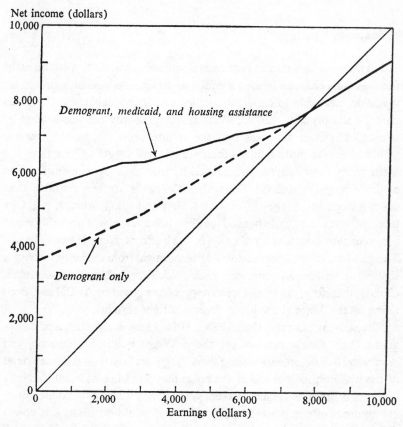

Sources: Same as Figure 4-7.

rate of one-third. Because of social security taxes and unreimbursed work-related expenses, such a family faces a tax rate of well over 50 percent on the first $3,000 of earnings, and more modest rates above that point. Compared with the Long plan, under the demogrant the tax rates are higher on workers with very low wages, lower on workers with low to moderate wages ($4,000 to $5,600), and higher on moderate-wage workers.

Once again, however, the tax rates rise quite high if the demogrant and reformed income tax are combined with federal housing and medical assistance and any other income-tested benefits. They come to over 70 percent for all workers earning $7,220 or less who are eligible for housing and medicaid as well as demogrants.

Summary

All three welfare reform proposals discussed in this section would assist families with children headed by men as well as by women; demogrants would be available to childless couples and individuals also. The plans contrast sharply with AFDC, which serves primarily families headed by women. The high tax rates that the reform proposals would generate would affect far more families than are affected by AFDC tax rates because many more families are headed by men than by women. Existing evidence suggests that families with male heads are less sensitive than other groups to changes in tax rates. Any reduction in work effort by principal earners in male-headed families, however, would probably cause more concern than would reduction in work effort by female family heads. The prospect of complete and visible withdrawal from the labor force of a significant number of prime-age males would probably doom any plan. Clearly, therefore, the work incentive problems posed by AFDC and, even more, by the major alternatives, deserve serious scrutiny.

The striking tax rates that AFDC, H.R. 1, the Long plan, and demogrants share should not obscure the profound political, economic, and administrative differences among them. They are based on different views of the welfare problem and of the poor; they would provide substantially different benefits and reach different people; they would entail quite different amounts of administrative discretion and would distribute this power differently. Nevertheless, the work disincentive problem caused by high marginal tax rates arises under all these highly disparate programs.

This problem arises because the welfare system includes not only cash assistance but various in-kind benefits as well. To make these benefits available on equitable criteria based on economic need will inevitably be costly and will expose increasing numbers of families to the complexities of multiple benefits, to high tax rates, and to serious work disincentives. Unless the various in-kind programs are integrated with cash assistance, the work incentive problem cannot be solved. The next chapter reviews a number of technical proposals to improve these programs and integrate them with cash assistance.

CHAPTER FIVE

Alternative Ways to Increase Work Effort

The government can increase work incentives by making work pay or by making the failure to work illegal or unbearable.

The simplest way of making the failure to work unbearable would be to terminate all forms of federal assistance. Almost no one seriously advocates casting off the blind, the disabled, or the aged poor, but some doubt the wisdom or morality of aiding others. If aid to families with dependent children (AFDC) were terminated, heads of families with children would be forced to seek aid from state governments, private charities, or relatives, to work, or to starve. Few doubt that labor force participation of welfare recipients would rise if welfare were ended.

Despite periodic efforts to cut welfare rolls, this method of increasing work incentives enjoys little support. The record of public assistance clearly indicates that however anxious Congress and state legislatures may be to strip benefits from welfare cheaters or from those thought capable of working, most legislators are prepared to aid large numbers of the poor, particularly those who have tried sincerely but failed to find work.

Administrative Requirements

Once a welfare system exists, a fundamental decision must be made whether to handle the problem of work incentives by inducing recipients to work or by requiring them to do so as a condition for aid. This decision implies certain choices in determining eligibility and benefits. On the one hand, eligibility might be based solely on the economic circumstances of applicants. The present system does not follow this course; it excludes childless households and most families headed by men, partly on the ground that adults in such households have no excuse for not working. Late in 1971 Congress stipulated that all adult welfare recipients, except mothers of preschool children, must register for work or training. H.R. 1 contained a similar requirement. Such work requirements are attractive to those who believe that welfare recipients are slackers, and especially to those, like mothers of preschool children now in the labor force, who find work a chore and inconvenience and wonder why others should be spared.

Unfortunately, administrative requirements are unlikely to solve the work incentive problem unless work also pays. The lessons of other income support programs are instructive. From the very beginning recipients of unemployment insurance have had to accept reasonable job offers or face loss of benefits. To prevent abuses, however, the law contained a "suitability test": Jobs had to be appropriate to the skills and training of the unemployed person and within reasonable commuting distance. In practice, many available jobs are found to be "unsuitable" for the unemployed worker. College graduates have not been required to dig ditches, nor grammar school graduates to program computers. Furthermore, the fact that the unemployed have often outnumbered the available jobs has made it even harder to determine whether the applicant turned away by an employer really tried to get the job. In any case, nearly anyone can arrange to be rejected if he is disinclined to accept the job.

It would be even harder to enforce a work requirement on recipients of public assistance, food stamps, housing assistance, or medicaid than on recipients of unemployment insurance. On the average, people served by these programs are less well educated and have fewer marketable skills than those served by unemployment insurance. In the absence of persuasive incentives, an employer is less likely to inform governmental agencies of job openings for welfare recipients. Consequently, such applicants probably will outnumber available jobs. Moreover, they may intentionally or unintentionally behave so as not to be hired or, once hired, to be fired. Unless it were possible to distinguish those who can work but refuse to do so, from all other recipients of assistance, a work requirement would be ineffectual on those who resolved to evade it. How to make this distinction raises difficulties that are probably insuperable.

For example, should a carwasher who is laid off during a rainy spell be required to take a different job? ... What should be done about an ice cream vendor in the winter? What kind of work will be defined as "suitable" for a mother with no previous work experience, and what kind of job will she be required to accept to maintain her portion of . . . benefits? These questions are intended to suggest the difficulty of administering a work test, especially for a population of marginal workers whose work patterns are typically unstable.[1]

Removal of the "suitability test" would simplify many of these problems. Administrators would not have to make complex judgments, for example, about the reasonableness of requiring a particular recipient to commute a particular distance to a particular job. The Talmadge amendment requiring AFDC recipients to register for work and training does not contain a suitability test. Neither did H.R. 1 or the Long plan.

But some observers fear that work requirements, even those circumscribed by a suitability test, would foster administrative abuse. In small towns and rural areas, particularly those with one employer or highly seasonal demands for labor, the requirement could be administered to foster an abundant labor supply, to hold down wages, or to maintain racial subjugation.[2] Such critics allege that a work requirement would create a pool of workers forced by the threat of starvation to take any job, however repulsive, at any wage, however low; that supporters of work requirements want, among other things, to ensure a plentiful supply of cheap, menial labor;[3] in short, that a work requirement will enslave the poor by requiring that they do the bidding of the authorities to get food for their children. Removal of the suitability test would create greater opportunities for abuse. Many critics oppose a work requirement, also, from a belief that the government of a country as wealthy as the United States is morally obliged to prevent starvation or gross poverty and that cash assistance should be available to the poor as a matter of right.

The criticism that a work requirement would be abused is obviously serious. But the criticisms stressed here allege that, if work does not pay,

1. D. Lee Bawden, Glen C. Cain, and Leonard J. Hausman, "The Family Assistance Plan: An Analysis and Evaluation," *Public Policy,* Vol. 19 (Spring 1971), p. 345.

2. The AFDC system is alleged to operate in this manner in much of the South and in rural California.

3. The proposal of Senator Russell B. Long to permit tax deductions for wages paid to domestics who would otherwise be on welfare lends credence to this allegation, as does Governor Lester Maddox's statement that if the family assistance plan passed, "You're not going to be able to find anyone willing to work as maids or janitors or housekeepers" (*Wall Street Journal,* December 15, 1970, as cited by Irene Lurie in "Interstate Differentials in Welfare Benefits," University of Wisconsin, Institute for Research on Poverty, 1972; processed, p. 1).

a work requirement in most places and times would be ineffectual and inoperative, a costly and largely futile effort to compel the poor to behave in ways contrary to their own self-interest. It is unimaginable that a large bureaucracy would be capable of sifting millions of individual cases, each fraught with special problems, needs, and ambiguity, all requiring judgment if not wisdom. To inspire hard work is a laudable goal, but one not likely to be achieved through a work requirement without more authoritarian administration than most Americans are likely to accept.

Economic Incentives

The other way to create work incentives is to make work pay. The person who earns more must derive sufficient gain to make the extra work worthwhile. For some adults, including many recipients of welfare, work is an end in itself, a means to personal satisfaction and social status; such people will work for psychic gains even if the financial reward is small.[4] Other adults refuse work even if the gains are great; for them the rewards of leisure suffice. For many, however, the decision to report daily to a job that is neither repugnant nor very attractive may be influenced by economic considerations. In some cases the influence may be direct, in others, indirect, through peer-group pressures that in turn are shaped by economic influences. Whether the importance of economic incentives is real or only apparent, many political leaders believe that such incentives significantly affect work effort. In either case the success of efforts to reform welfare will be promoted by the creation of genuine work incentives in a restructured system.

The Negative Income Tax

For well over a decade economists have advocated introducing a negative income tax as an alternative to AFDC. Some have proposed that a negative income tax replace in-kind assistance as well.[5]

The negative income tax assures to all eligible households without other

4. For evidence that the motivation of the poor to work closely resembles that of other groups, see Leonard Goodwin, *Do The Poor Want to Work? A Social-Psychological Study of Work Orientations* (Brookings Institution, 1972).

5. For example, Milton Friedman initially favored the negative income tax as an alternative also for social security, unemployment insurance, and farm price supports; see his *Capitalism and Freedom* (University of Chicago Press, 1962), especially Chaps. 12 and 13.

income basic support related to family size. As earned income rises the family is subject to an implicit tax through reductions in support payments. The basic support levels and the implicit tax define the income range of eligible families.[6] The negative income tax may be restricted to certain groups, such as families with children. The amount of support may depend on family net worth as well as on income. In fact, the problems of creating a negative income tax parallel those of the (positive) personal income tax.[7]

In a trivial sense the United States already has a negative income tax: AFDC provides certain kinds of families a geographically variable guarantee whose implicit tax rate is 66⅔ percent of income over $360 per year with credit for taxes paid and work-related expenses. H.R. 1 and demogrants combined with tax reform are kinds of negative income taxes. The former was limited to families with children; the basic support level of $2,400 for a family of four was not geographically variable although states could have supplemented this payment; the implicit tax was 66⅔ percent of earnings over $720 per year without any credit for taxes paid or work-related expenses; it replaced AFDC and one form of commodity assistance, food stamps, but retained other forms of commodity assistance. Demogrants are payable to everyone: They guarantee $3,600 to a family of four, for example; the implicit tax rate is, say, 33⅓ percent on income; deductions or credits could be incorporated without altering the basic structure.

If AFDC, H.R. 1, or demogrants are viewed in this light, the issue is not whether to adopt a negative income tax but what features it should have to reinforce work incentives and to achieve more equitable eligibility standards and benefit levels. These plans also make clear that to advocate replacement of the existing system with a negative income tax is meaningless until one specifies the attributes of the assistance program one es-

6. For example, a plan that provides $3,000 for a family of four and that reduces benefits $1 for every $2 of earnings (a 50 percent tax rate) will provide benefits to all four-person families with earnings of less than $6,000. The negative income tax is "negative" in the sense that the *average* tax rate is negative; that is, a transfer is paid rather than a tax collected. Most popularly discussed negative income taxes have high *positive marginal* tax rates on increments to earnings. See Christopher Green, *Negative Taxes and the Poverty Problem* (Brookings Institution, 1967), pp. 62–67, for a discussion of the relationship among the guarantee level, the implicit tax rate, and the eligibility ceiling.

7. James Tobin, Joseph A. Pechman, and Peter M. Mieszkowski discuss these problems at length and propose solutions to them in "Is a Negative Income Tax Practical?" *Yale Law Journal,* Vol. 77 (November 1967), pp. 1–27. (Brookings Reprint 142.)

pouses. Then the discussion can turn to these attributes and need not center on an empty, but frequently emotional, debate about the desirability of negative income taxes.

The figures above that relate to AFDC, H.R. 1, and demogrants make clear that a negative income tax like these plans does not solve the work incentive problem. At least three features contribute to that failure: the high implicit tax rate contained in these forms of the negative income tax, the failure to terminate in-kind benefits or to integrate them with the cash assistance program, and the failure to take income and payroll taxes and work-related expenses into account in computing family income.[8] The remainder of this chapter will review alternative methods of amending these three features of assistance programs to improve work incentives.

Reducing the Tax Rate

The most obvious way to improve work incentives appears to be to lower the implicit tax rate under cash assistance—from 66⅔ percent to, say, 50, 40, or 33⅓ percent. A 66⅔ percent tax permits the worker to keep $1 when he earns $3; a 50 percent tax lets him keep $1.50; a 33⅓ percent tax, $2.

Unfortunately, this approach is exceedingly costly; but what is worse, it doesn't work. The tax rate under the illustrative demogrant system is only 33⅓ percent. The tax rate embodied in the Long plan is even lower over certain income brackets for low-wage workers. When combined with in-kind assistance, however, the rates swell to 70 percent or more (see Figures 4-7 and 4-8). For this reason the simple approach of cutting the tax rate under cash assistance is inadequate to make work pay. No matter how far Congress moves to build work incentives into cash assistance, the effort will fail unless in-kind assistance is also reformed.[9]

Lowering the tax rates for the lower-income brackets requires that assistance be paid to families in the middle-income brackets; that step vastly increases the cost of assistance and it spreads the work incentive problem widely because it exposes the families to much higher marginal tax rates than they face under current law. Even if the effect on work effort of each family is small, the total effect may be considerable. Because

---

8. H.R. 1 would have allowed day care costs to be deducted.

9. For these reasons, proposals, such as that introduced by Senator Gaylord Nelson (*Congressional Record,* daily edition, April 5, 1972, pp. S5385–86), to limit the reduction in cash assistance under H.R. 1 to 50 percent of earnings in excess of $720, do not materially alleviate the work disincentive problem.

of the large number and high labor force participation of families in such brackets, the increase in their marginal tax rate may well cost more—in terms of their reduced work effort—than is gained by reducing the tax rate on low-income families.

"Cashing Out" Commodity Assistance

One approach would be to replace, or "cash out," in-kind assistance with more generous cash assistance. This position receives support both from those who believe that the federal government has no business telling people how to spend their incomes and from those who feel that federal efforts to influence the composition of private outlays often fail or produce unintended consequences.[10] It is not possible simultaneously to cash out in-kind benefits for all recipients of cash assistance and to keep down implicit tax rates without extending assistance to a large fraction of the American population, thus vastly increasing total benefits and substantially raising taxes on the remainder of the population to finance them. The cost of a $2,400 guarantee with a 50 percent tax rate is nearly one-half greater than that of a $2,400 guarantee with a 66⅔ percent tax, and one with a 33⅓ percent tax costs more than four times as much. Lowering the tax rate costs so much partly because most families who receive some assistance when the tax rate is high receive more when it is low. More important, reducing the tax rate increases the number of families assisted. A $2,400 guarantee (with $720 of earnings disregarded) reaches families with earnings up to $4,320 when the tax rate is 66⅔ percent, $5,520 when the tax rate is 50 percent, $7,920 when the tax rate is 33⅓ percent. Lowering the tax rate opens up eligibility in earnings brackets that are more and more thickly populated.

Furthermore, alongside its grudging willingness to give the poor money, Congress has repeatedly expressed through legislation a desire to improve housing or provide free medical assistance or subsidized food. The initial passage of assistance in kind requires no explanation more profound than that legislators are more pained to know that children are hungry, that the sick are neglected, or that squalid housing blights their city than they are about less obtrusive or disturbing forms of deprivation. To the extent that

10. For an example of the first group, see Friedman, *Capitalism and Freedom,* Chap. 11; representative of the second are Gilbert Y. Steiner, *The State of Welfare* (Brookings Institution, 1971), Chap. 1, and Theodore J. Lowi, *The End of Liberalism: Ideology, Policy, and the Crisis of Public Authority* (W. W. Norton, 1969), especially Chap. 9.

those who pay taxes feel more concerned about the health or housing than about the clothing or recreation of the poor, the case for commodity assistance, as opposed to general cash assistance is strengthened.[11]

Especially if some motives for in-kind assistance are unrelated to the welfare of recipients—for example, reduction of food stocks, in the case of food distribution—cash assistance is hardly an answer. At an equally mundane level, the existence of housing, medical, and food assistance means that congressional committees, subcommittees, and their staffs, and federal agencies have a special concern with these programs. While they may support amendments in them, they are quite likely to resist repeal. Whether based on parochial self-interest or on special knowledge, the views of these powerful groups must be recognized.

Recent actions of Congress suggest that assistance in kind can be curtailed in some circumstances. Both H.R. 1 and the Long plan would have denied food assistance to recipients of the basic federal guarantee. The prospects and the desirability of similarly restricting housing and medical assistance to the poor are far more questionable, however, largely because no income maintenance scheme in sight would cause recipients voluntarily to buy the quantity of housing and medical services that federal legislation indicates the nation views as "basic." Furthermore, most housing assistance is provided on dwellings built with the guarantee of government subsidies for up to fifty years; the subsidies on existing units cannot in fact be terminated.

Cash or In-kind Benefits—Not Both

Recipients of cash assistance might be required to treat the value of in-kind benefits as part of that assistance. For example, a family eligible for $2,400 in cash that receives a housing subsidy of, say, $1,000 might be paid only $1,400 in cash. Alternatively, the cash grant might be reduced by some fraction of the value of the housing subsidy. Medicaid or day care subsidies might be treated similarly.

This approach would reduce the aggregate value of benefits for some families now eligible under two or more programs, especially in relatively generous states. It would confront them with the painful choice between

11. See Henry J. Aaron and George M. von Furstenberg, "The Inefficiency of Transfers in Kind: The Case of Housing Assistance," *Western Economic Journal*, Vol. 9 (June 1971), pp. 184–91 (Brookings Reprint 210); Harold M. Hochman and James D. Rodgers, "Pareto Optimal Redistribution," *American Economic Review*, Vol. 59 (September 1969), pp. 542–57.

surrendering health or housing subsidies or paying a disproportionate share of income to retain them. If the family had to pay full cost for them, most would refuse them and retain their expenditure options. As a result the very poorest families, with no money income other than cash assistance, would be compelled to give up medicaid or subsidized housing; those who received little or no cash assistance because of outside income, but who were eligible for in-kind benefits, would opt for them. The fact that the poor would be unable to afford "standard" housing or comprehensive health insurance would mean that many of the very poorest families would have housing or medical care below national standards. It is doubtful whether an explicit policy of excluding those most in need from health or housing assistance would command widespread support.

A Tax Ceiling

If commodity assistance continues, some method must be found to prevent implicit tax rates under these programs and cash assistance from cumulating into intolerable work disincentives. A possible approach is to use *one* program to guarantee each recipient under *any* program that the cumulative tax rates to which he is exposed will not exceed some maximum, such as 50, 60, or 66⅔ percent. The most obvious candidate for this role is cash assistance.

This approach could work as follows: A family that was eligible for cash assistance only would face, say, a $0.50 reduction in assistance for each additional $1 in earnings—a 50 percent tax. Another family, which received in addition housing assistance that was cut by $0.25 for each additional $1 in earnings, would have its cash assistance cut by only $0.25, making a $0.50 reduction overall. Alternatively, the implicit tax rate on families receiving benefits under two or more programs might be allowed to exceed slightly the tax on families receiving cash assistance alone. In the example, when earnings rise $1 and housing assistance thus falls by $0.25, cash assistance might be reduced by, say, $0.35, making a 60 percent tax.

This approach appears to permit solution of the work incentives problem without revising assistance in kind. It would in one motion assure that poor households would not confront tax rates above some agreed maximum. Unfortunately, it would create serious problems for federal-state fiscal relations. Moreover, the costs of this solution are likely to approach those of cashing out commodity benefits. A simple example illustrates the problem. Assume that the basic federal guarantee is similar to that contained in H.R. 1—$2,400 per year for a family of four; that the first $720 per year of earnings will be disregarded in computing cash or commodity assistance; and that the total tax rate on earnings above $720 will not exceed 50 percent. Consider three four-member families, *A, B,* and *C.* Family *A* earns $4,000 and receives no housing assistance in a low-benefit state that does not supplement the basic guarantee but provides modest health benefits worth an average of $200 per year. Family *B* lives in the same state and earns $9,000. Family *C* earns $9,000 but lives in a high-benefit state that pays a supplement of $1,800 per year and medical benefits worth $1,000 per year to a family of four with no earnings; family *C* also lives in subsidized housing worth $1,800 per year, for which it pays one-fourth of net income. Family *A* receives benefits worth $960 and would receive some until its earnings rose to $5,920. Family *B* receives no assistance. Family *C* receives benefits worth $1,860 and would receive some until its income reached $12,720.

This system would encourage not only the poor, but also the middle class, to migrate from low-benefit to high-benefit states. AFDC has been criticized for encouraging such migration among the poor, a group known to be far less mobile than the middle class.

Furthermore, in order to enforce a maximum tax rate, the federal government would have to restrict the rates states could apply on earnings in computing state supplementary payments. If earnings led first to a reduction in state supplementary payments and then to a reduction in the federal basic guarantee, states could bring about a vast increase in federal transfers to their residents at relatively modest costs in higher state transfers. State legislators would feel an enormous incentive to raise supplements which would impose only moderate costs on the state treasury but would force the federal government to assist the lower-middle- and middle-income families at the expense of the nation at large. If earnings led to a reduction first in the federal payment and then in state supplements (as under H.R. 1), the cost to the states from liberalization of the federal guarantee would be substantial, unless they curtailed supplementary payments. Such a reaction by a state would create hardship for its recipients of cash assistance who did not also receive in-kind assistance. Federal increases in, say, housing assistance might trigger equal declines in state-financed cash assistance; recipients of both would lose some control over how they spend their assistance, but recipients solely of cash assistance would clearly suffer.

In summary, federal efforts to put a ceiling on the implicit tax rate on recipients of assistance will create or perpetuate problems—insupportable costs, or inter- or intrastate inequities—that are nearly as serious as those it solves, particularly if states pay widely differing amounts of supplementary cash assistance and if other types of assistance cover some, but not all, recipients of cash assistance.

Integration of Methods of Computing Taxes

One flaw produced by the disconnected history of assistance programs is easily repaired. Unfortunately, the gains would be small. The flaw is that the implicit tax rates under each program do not always take account of those under other programs. For example, rents in low-rent public housing or in rental-assistance housing, and mortgage payments in homeownership-assistance housing, are based on cash income including public assistance and earnings; no allowance is made for federal or state income taxes paid, although certain deductions are permitted. Under H.R. 1, cash assistance and the medicaid deductible would have been based on gross earnings without regard for payroll taxes or federal and state income taxes (let alone work-related expenses); housing benefits would have taken no account of medicaid benefits or of the implicit tax on them. The Long plan would have imposed a premium for medicaid based on gross earnings rather than net income.

One consequence of this lack of coordination is that tax rates can easily cumulate to more than 100 percent—more easily under H.R. 1 than under the existing system, the Long plan, or demogrants. Another consequence is that two families receiving the same gross amount of assistance under the current system may be in quite different situations after the implicit taxes have been netted out.[12]

12. Family *A* receives $2,400 per year in cash assistance, has no earnings, lives in subsidized housing with a fair market rent of $1,800 per year for which it must pay $600 in rent (one-fourth of income), and is permitted to buy food stamps worth $1,296 at a cost of $636. Its benefits in cash and commodities total $4,260. Family *B*, also without earnings, lives in a state with higher benefits and receives $4,260 in cash assistance but does not live in subsidized housing. Both families receive cash and commodity assistance worth $4,260 although Family *B* has greater choice than Family *A* in planning its expenditures. Then, both families find part-time work and earn $3,000 (in addition to the $360 exclusion, work-related expenses, and taxes). The cash assistance to family *A* declines to $400, its rent rises to $850, and the cost of its food stamps to $924; its total benefits decline to $1,722 for a combined tax rate of 85 percent. The cash assistance to family *B* declines to $2,260. It gets approximately $500 more net income for working than Family *A* because it faces only one tax rate. H.R. 1 would have aggravated this problem: Under its provisions a family eligible for cash assistance, medicaid, and housing assistance could have faced tax rates as high as 130 percent.

This problem cannot be solved unless a single tax rate is applied to the sum of all benefits or all benefit schedules are geographically uniform. It can be mitigated, however, if the rates are applied sequentially to net resources—the sum of all cash assistance and earnings plus the market value of assistance in kind less all taxes, fees, and charges. This procedure prevents the most serious work disincentive—the circumstance in which an increase in earnings reduces a family's net income. To illustrate, as earnings rise, a four-person family must pay social security payroll taxes from the first dollar of earnings, federal income taxes on earnings in excess of $4,300 (if the family uses the low-income allowance), and state income taxes for its earnings level. Cash assistance should be based on earnings net of these taxes, rather than gross earnings (unless, as in many states, a full credit is given for taxes paid). The sum of net earnings and cash assistance equals disposable cash income. The net value of, say, medicaid should be added to disposable cash income. The charges imposed for, say, assisted housing (or the size of a housing allowance) should depend on the sum of disposable cash income and the net value of medical coverage. And so on for any other commodity assistance, such as subsidized day care.[13]

This arrangement would assure only that the cumulative tax rate did not exceed 100 percent. Unless the rates were kept to moderate levels the cumulative rate might be so close to 100 percent as to leave assistance recipients only meager recompense for work.[14]

---

13. Symbolically, let t_i represent the implicit tax rate for assistance of form i ($i = 1, \ldots, n$); D_i the amount of income disregarded in computing the benefit; and A_i the amount of assistance when family disposable income including net transfers is D_i. Then family income after the ith transfer program, y_i, is equal to $y_{i-1} + A_i - t_i(y_{i-1} - D_i)$, where $y_0 = E$, earnings. An increase in earnings must raise y_i if $t_i < 1$ for all i, since $dy_i/dE = (dy_i/dy_{i-1}) (dy_{i-1}/dy_{i-2}) \ldots (dy_1/dy_0) = (1 - t_i) (1 - t_{i-1}) \ldots (1 - t_1)$, which is necessarily positive.

14. To illustrate, a worker who paid payroll taxes of 5 percent and federal income taxes of 14 percent, and who suffered a reduction in cash assistance of 66⅔ percent, in medical assistance of 20 percent, and in housing assistance of 25 percent, would face a cumulative tax rate of 84 percent, thus: $(1 - 0.05 - 0.14) (1 - 0.66) (1 - 0.2) (1 - 0.25) = 0.165$.

For further examples of how to integrate tax rates under various programs, see Thad W. Mirer, "Notes on Schemes for Integrating Welfare Programs (paper prepared for delivery at the Joint Economic Committee-Institute for Research on Poverty Conference on Income Maintenance Programs, University of Wisconsin, July 1972; processed).

Program Redesign

Cash Assistance

AFDC, H.R. 1, and demogrants all guarantee a basic payment to eligible families with no earnings or other income and they all impose a positive marginal tax on earnings. Indeed, the high positive marginal tax rates under cash and commodity assistance are jointly responsible for the work disincentive problem. As far as benefit and tax schedules are concerned, no distinction is made between the employable and unemployable. These plans are unitary. The Long plan would have continued AFDC for those not required to work and would introduce a wage subsidy for those deemed employable. AFDC contains a relatively high benefit and a high tax rate; the Long plan provided no benefit when there were no earnings, but contained genuinely negative tax rates. The Long plan was binary.[15]

In a binary system families may be able to choose the part of the system into which they fall. Under the Long plan, for example, a woman could have stayed under the AFDC system by allowing no more than six years between births. A man who cannot find private employment and rejects the public employment offered to him, or who earns less than he thinks his family needs, could leave his family, thereby making them eligible for AFDC. There is no evidence that significant numbers of families respond to the similar incentives in the AFDC system. But the lack of evidence has not prevented critics of AFDC from condemning the system for these faults.[16] Those, including Senator Long, who fault the AFDC system for these incentives should not look to measures like H.R. 1 or the Long plan for redress.[17]

The preceding comparison of AFDC and the Long plan illustrates the kind of problems that may arise within any binary system if families have discretion over their own benefits. This possibility is particularly disturbing

---

15. In principle, it would be possible to have three or more plans for separate groups. The separate programs for the aged, blind, and disabled may be viewed in this light.

16. On this subject, see Steiner, *State of Welfare*, especially Chap. 3.

17. H.R. 1 raised the same issue in more acute form. After 1974, mothers without children under the age of three were to be required to accept jobs or training as a condition for benefits. While the justice of this requirement is debatable, the fact remains that any mother who felt deeply she should be with her three-year-old, or who simply didn't want to work, could follow her inclination by having another child.

when it involves decisions about such basic matters as marriage or cohabitation and the number of children.

Despite these problems of binary systems, experts on income maintenance remain attracted to them, because the problems of the family with no potential earner differ significantly from those of the family with an unemployed or low-skilled worker. Some have proposed wage subsidies; some, earnings subsidies.[18]

Proponents of wage and earnings subsidies focus on the sensitive work incentive question. The case for wage supplements instead of earnings subsidies rests on a politically and economically significant distinction between the implicit tax rate on increases in earnings due to an increase in hours worked on the one hand and in hourly wages on the other.[19] Public statements suggest that congressmen are concerned more about the person who does not work at all than about the person who works but refuses an increase in wages. An assistance program that applied a lower tax rate to increased earnings due to a rise in hours worked than to those from increased hourly wages would meet a politically relevant concern.

Table 5-1 illustrates such a plan. It shows the benefits payable to a family of four for various numbers of hours worked and hourly wages. The benefit for a family with no earnings is $2,400, the same amount provided in H.R. 1 and assured to public employees under the Long plan. Workers can earn $2,133 net of taxes without loss of benefits if net earnings are $1.60 per hour but only $593 if they earn $4 per hour. Each employee receives an allowance for work expenses of 30 cents per hour worked up to a maximum of $450. The implicit tax rate on net earnings due to increases in hours worked for a worker employed at the minimum wage ranges from zero for workers employed less than 1,333 hours to 30 per-

18. For an example of the wage subsidy proposal, see Richard J. Zeckhauser, "Optimal Mechanisms for Income Transfer," *American Economic Review,* Vol. 61 (June 1971), pp. 324–34; also, in "An Alternative to the Nixon Income Maintenance Plan," *Public Interest,* No. 19 (Spring 1970), pp. 120–30, Zeckhauser and Peter Schuck propose a wage subsidy equal to half the difference between the worker's hourly wage and $3.00 per hour. An example of the earnings subsidy proposal appears in Robert Haveman and Robert Lampman, "Two Alternatives to FAP's Treatment of the Working Poor" (Institute for Research on Poverty, April 1971; processed). These authors suggest a 100 percent earnings subsidy on earnings up to $1,300 per year for a four-person family, recaptured by a 50 percent tax on earnings between $1,300 and $3,900 per year. Haveman and Lampman advocate a binary system.

19. The Zeckhauser-Schuck wage supplement applies a 50 percent tax on increased earnings due to rises in wage rates and pays a subsidy at a rate that ranges from 44 percent (at the minimum wage, $1.60 per hour) to zero (at $3.00 per hour) for additional hours worked.

Table 5-1. Work Incentive Benefits under Unitary Formula with Maximum Annual Benefits of $2,400 for a Family of Four, by Hourly Earnings and Hours Worked

All amounts in dollars

Hourly earnings net of payroll and income taxes	Hours worked per year					
	100	250	500	1,000	1,500	2,000
1.60	2,400	2,400	2,400	2,400	2,370	2,130
1.80	2,400	2,400	2,400	2,340	2,190	1,890
2.00	2,400	2,400	2,400	2,220	2,010	1,650
2.20	2,400	2,400	2,370	2,100	1,830	1,410
2.40	2,400	2,400	2,310	1,980	1,650	1,170
2.60	2,400	2,400	2,250	1,860	1,470	930
2.80	2,400	2,400	2,190	1,740	1,290	690
3.00	2,400	2,385	2,130	1,620	1,110	450
3.20	2,400	2,355	2,070	1,500	930	210
3.40	2,400	2,325	2,010	1,380	750	0
3.60	2,400	2,295	1,950	1,260	570	0
3.80	2,400	2,265	1,890	1,140	390	0
4.00	2,400	2,235	1,830	1,020	210	0
4.20	2,400	2,205	1,770	900	30	0
4.40	2,400	2,175	1,710	780	0	0
4.60	2,400	2,145	1,650	660	0	0
4.80	2,400	2,115	1,590	540	0	0

Source: Prepared by author. The formula for computing the benefits is $B = B' + W$, where $B' = 2640 - 0.3H$ ($1.60) $- 0.6H$ ($E - 1.60) and $W = 0.3H$. The symbol B represents benefits; B', intermediate benefits; W, work expenses allowances; H, hours worked; E, hourly earnings. B and W are constrained as follows: Maximum benefit = $2,400, minimum benefit = $0, and maximum work allowance = $450.

cent for those employed more than 1,500 hours. For workers earning $3.00 per hour, the tax rate ranges from zero for those who work less than 235 hours to 44 percent for those who work more than 1,500 hours. Benefits would be reduced by 60 percent of additional earnings due solely to increases in average hourly earnings.

This formula encourages earners to work additional hours, a decision over which some workers, particularly women and casual laborers, exercise considerable discretion. A major shortcoming is that it provides smaller—though still positive—incentives to accept or seek employment at higher wages. A maximum of, say, 2,000 hours (that is, year-round full-time employment) would be used in computing benefits. Such a rule would subject overtime wages and earnings by secondary workers to the 60 percent tax.

This formula offers low-wage workers great incentive to supplement the federal grant with earnings, and is likely to attract low-wage and part-time workers into the labor force. It also assures a substantial average wage to higher-wage workers, who must choose between full-time employment and none at all because of job rules.[20] By exposing low earnings to no tax, and modest increases in earnings from working longer hours to a low tax, this type of benefit formula promotes work effort by low-wage, part-time, and marginal workers who are sensitive to the tax rate, at the same time that it offers a large *average* gain to higher-wage, regular workers who have been shown to be less sensitive to marginal tax rates.

This formula is purely illustrative. Alternatives could be designed to reward more generously hours worked by high-wage workers, to encourage overtime work or secondary workers, or to reduce the implicit tax on increased hourly earnings. The essential characteristic is that this formula differentiates between hours worked and hourly earnings in determining benefit levels. The chief consequence is that, even if their total earnings are the same, a worker who is employed more hours at a lower hourly wage than another worker will receive more cash assistance. As a result fewer workers would withdraw completely from the labor force than would be induced to do so by plans such as H.R. 1, which subjects to high tax rates increases in wages due to additional hours worked.

A benefit formula that distinguishes changes in earnings related to hours worked from those due to wage rates requires two sets of implicit taxes and data on both hours worked and wage rates. Such a formula may encourage collusion between employers and employees to understate hourly earnings and overstate hours. To reduce the problem, earnings of less than, say, $1,200 per year might be deemed to have been earned at the minimum wage. A benefit formula based solely on earnings avoids this problem, but fails to distinguish between hours worked and wages earned in the determination of benefits.

The benefit formula shown in Table 5-1 is not a wage subsidy, since benefits do not at any point increase with earnings. It is, however, a unitary system. This fact means that all people within the system are treated alike, thereby reducing incentives to alter family arrangements.

---

20. A worker who earns $5.00 per hour gross wages will lose only about $62.50 in transfers for his first $1,187.50 of net after-tax earnings. After payment of taxes, the net hourly wage of such a worker who heads a family of four is $4.75; 250 hours of employment yields net earnings of $1,175.50.

Housing

Federal housing programs provide very large benefits, averaging approximately $1,000 per year per family. Most beneficiaries are families with incomes near or beyond the income limits for cash assistance. There are two distinct reasons why housing might be subsidized. First, the nation has declared repeatedly through legislation its interest in assuring decent housing for all. The methods it has adopted to achieve this objective have contained inefficiencies.[21] This paper has pointed out how they also have contributed to work disincentives. Second, variations in housing costs are the major cause of interregional differences in the cost of living. Accordingly, housing allowances should supplement cash assistance. To remove regional disparities, the supplement could vary from zero in the lowest-cost areas to an amount equal to the difference between housing costs there and in the highest-cost areas.

Existing housing programs pose work disincentives because families are expected to spend 20 to 25 percent of income on assisted units, with the government making up the difference between this amount and full costs. Since the subsidies are tied to particular units, the cost of housing to assisted families rises with their income, but they do not have the option of moving to better housing. By defraying a portion of the rent or housing costs of low-income households so that aid rises with housing expenditure but declines with income, the nation could better foster its goal of good housing without inflicting work disincentives as serious as those operating today. It would be entirely reasonable for this form of housing assistance to extend beyond the income range eligible for general income support since the declared interest in housing standards (in contrast with the silence about adequate provision of many other goods) implies society's greater concern with adequate housing.

Table 5-2 presents a housing allowance, based on income and housing outlays, that provides up to $600 per household. This amount is much below average assistance available to the minority of low-income households eligible under existing housing programs, but it is presumed to be generally available. The housing assistance formula is constructed so that households with $2,500 in net income that spend one-fifth of their own resources on housing receive $400 in housing allowances. The government would pay 50 percent of additional housing costs up to a maximum that would de-

---

21. See Henry J. Aaron, *Shelter and Subsidies: Who Benefits from Federal Housing Policies?* (Brookings Institution, 1972).

Table 5-2. Annual Housing Allowance under Formula with $600 Maximum and Family Housing Expenditure from Own Resources, by Selected Incomes

All amounts in dollars; family expenditure in parentheses

Total housing outlays	Disposable resources					
	2,500 or less	3,500	4,500	5,500	6,500	7,500
500	200	100	0	0	0	0
	(300)	(400)	(500)	(500)	(500)	(500)
700	300	200	100	0	0	0
	(400)	(500)	(600)	(700)	(700)	(700)
900	400	300	200	100	0	0
	(500)	(600)	(700)	(800)	(900)	(900)
1,100	500	400	300	200	100	0
	(600)	(700)	(800)	(900)	(1,000)	(1,100)
1,300	600	500	400	300	200	100
	(700)	(800)	(900)	(1,000)	(1,100)	(1,200)
1,500	600	500	400	300	200	100
	(900)	(1,000)	(1,100)	(1,200)	(1,300)	(1,400)
1,800	600	500	400	300	200	100
	(1,200)	(1,300)	(1,400)	(1,500)	(1,600)	(1,700)

Source: Prepared by author. For families with resources of $2,500 per year or less and housing cost of H, benefits $B_H^* = 0.5\ (H - \$100)$. B_H^* (maximum) $= \$600$. For families with higher annual money resources, Y, and housing expenditure H, the benefit is $B_H = B_H^* - 0.1\ (Y - \$2,500)$.

cline with income, from $600 per year for a family with $2,500 per year total income to nothing for a family with $8,500 per year income. No family would face a housing tax of greater than 10 percent of disposable income. The effective tax rate on earnings would be considerably lower, since disposable income would rise less rapidly than earnings.

Medical Care

Medical care raises the same tax issues as does housing assistance. The "notch" in the present medicaid formula, the 33⅓ percent implicit tax contained in H.R. 1, and the 20 percent premium for medicaid in the Long plan create formidable work disincentives. The limitation of these programs to the poor contributes to their peculiar design. The need to curtail benefits sharply as income rises would be reduced if medical assistance for the poor were imbedded in a broader health protection plan.

It is possible to design comprehensive health insurance schemes that establish premiums graduated with respect to income, yet that impose far more modest tax rates than does H.R. 1. For example, the national health insurance program proposed by Feldstein, Friedman, and Luft would cover all families and individuals, and would involve a premium, a deductible (the amount that must be paid before the insurer begins to pay any share of the medical expense), and coinsurance, a portion of medical costs above the deductible, all varying with income.[22] The implicit tax rate in their formula would vary according to income, family size, and gross costs of medical care. For a family of four with $3,000 in income and $500 in medical care costs, the implicit tax rate would be 8 percent. If income were $10,000 and medical costs were $1,000 the tax rate would be 10 percent. If total resources (earnings plus benefits) are used as the base, the tax rate works out to considerably less. According to Feldstein and his coworkers, this plan would not be self-financing. General revenues or earmarked taxes of $9.5 billion would be necessary to supplement income from premiums, deductibles, and coinsurance if these charges were based on the ordinary definition of income. The cost would be higher if these charges were based on net family resources.

Program Redesign—Cumulative Effect

If cash, housing, and medical assistance were awarded according to the formulas just described and if the tax rates were imposed sequentially, the basic benefit for a family of four with no outside earnings would be worth $3,410 (see Figures 5-1 and 5-2). Some cash benefits would be available until earnings reached $7,728.[23] Some housing assistance would be received by families of four until gross earnings exceeded $10,000 per year. The average value of medical care benefits for such a family would range from $414 for families with incomes below $2,000 per year to −$951 for families with incomes over $25,000 per year. Positive medical

---

22. See Martin Feldstein, Bernard Friedman, and Harold Luft, "Distributional Aspects of National Health Insurance Benefits and Finance," Discussion Paper 248 (Harvard University, Harvard Institute of Economic Research, August 1972; processed). The formula would require that families pay (1) a premium equal to $50 plus 1 percent of income in excess of $3,000 per year but less than $12,000 per year; (2) a deductible of $50 per adult plus $25 per child plus 5 percent of income in excess of $3,000 but less than $12,000 per year; and (3) a portion of medical costs in excess of the deductible equal to 8 percent plus 4 percent for each $1,000 of income up to $12,000.

23. This calculation presumes that the worker is employed 2,000 hours. Cash benefits would phase out at lower earnings if the worker were employed less than full time at a higher wage.

Figure 5-1. Tax Rates for a Family of Four under Proposed Alternative Assistance Programs

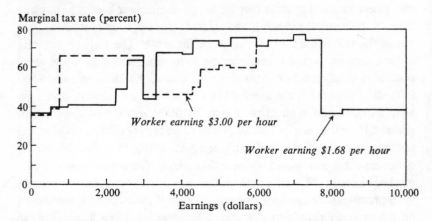

Marginal tax rate (percent)

Worker earning $3.00 per hour

Worker earning $1.68 per hour

Earnings (dollars)

Sources: Cash assistance is assumed to be distributed in the pattern shown in Table 5-1, housing assistance as in Table 5-2. Medical assistance is distributed according to the formula contained in note 22 above for a family with medical expenditure of $1,000.

Employees are assumed to incur work-related expenses, social security, and federal and state income taxes as in Figures 4-1 and 4-2.

benefits cease altogether at about $7,600. Removal of social security payroll taxes for low-income workers and further increases in their allowances would improve their work incentives somewhat.

The total benefit for a family with no earnings, $3,410, is much less than total benefits available today in the more generous states. This level is purely illustrative, but much larger universal benefits, worth $4,500 or $5,000 per year, are likely to be so costly as to be politically unacceptable. Some states doubtlessly would choose to supplement benefits at this level. They should be free to do so provided that the tax rates imposed by them do not thwart incentives. For example, states might be required to follow the basic formula shown in Table 5-1 but with state supplements added on. The costs of permissible supplements might be viewed as excessive by many states. A dilemma for the states would result—to maintain incentives at the cost of curtailing benefits for some families or to maintain benefits at high cost to the state.

Figure 5-1 shows the marginal tax rates facing two families. One earns $1.68 per hour gross; increases in earnings are due to increases in hours worked until the worker is employed 2,000 hours per year, and after that to increases in hourly wage rates. The other earns $3.00 per hour. As is apparent, the worker who earns more per hour faces a higher rate.

**Figure 5-2. Value of Benefits under Proposed Alternative
Assistance Programs, by Earnings Level**

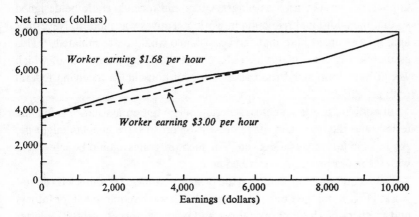

Net income (dollars)

Worker earning $1.68 per hour

Worker earning $3.00 per hour

Earnings (dollars)

Sources: Same as Figure 5-1.

Both workers have substantial work incentives, however. The low-wage
worker faces a tax rate averaging 44 percent if he works less than full time;
for the higher-wage worker the rate is 56 percent, but the increase in his
after-tax resources is larger than that of the low-wage worker. The low-
wage worker gains $1,878 from full-time employment after work-related
expenses are deducted and assistance is reduced; the high-wage worker
gains $2,630. Increases in earnings due to increases in hourly wages or to
overtime work would be exposed to higher tax rates. In other words, workers would lose more by curtailing (or gain more by increasing) work
hours, and relatively less from increasing or decreasing hourly earnings.

Conversion of the existing welfare system to the integrated, three-part
system described here would vastly improve equity and would substantially
raise work incentives for families now receiving cash assistance. It would
extend benefits to the working poor and lower-middle class. Along with
these benefits these groups would face tax rates that would be relatively
low only by comparison with those under AFDC or H.R. 1; they would be
far higher than those that now apply. Both the transfer and the increased
tax rates would tend to cause low-income workers to reduce work effort,
although it is impossible at this time to say by how much. Unlike demogrants, this system would not provide transfer or tax relief to middle-income workers.

Reform of the assistance system will create some new problems. The first question concerns the in-kind benefits not treated in this chapter. Continuation of the food stamp program would require yet another implicit tax on increased earnings. A food aid formula could be designed so that the additional reduction in work incentives was modest. Nevertheless, it is assumed here that food assistance would be terminated.[24] This assumption is consistent with H.R. 1 and the Long plan, both of which would have terminated food stamps for all households receiving federal cash assistance.

In addition to food stamps, federal college tuition assistance is income tested, and day care and other present or prospective benefits might be. An income test means a tax rate. All such programs should be integrated with the major programs described here.

The second problem concerns the proper treatment of adults who do not work. H.R. 1 and the Long plan established a work requirement for fathers and mothers of children over three and over six, respectively. The latter also guaranteed a public service job, newly created if necessary. The former approach, as argued earlier, is likely to be ineffective or repressive or both. The latter is likely to be extraordinarily difficult and costly to administer if the public employment opportunities are to be adequate to absorb all who become unemployed and needy over the business cycle. The size of this group fluctuates widely. If the number of jobs does not keep pace with the demand for them, the guarantee will be an empty gesture for some. The effort to provide public employment or to find jobs for the unemployed may well be a good investment of public funds. The propositions advanced here are that (a) such efforts are more likely to succeed the better work pays, and (b) under the best of circumstances they can reduce the scope of, but cannot replace, cash assistance.

Summary

By now it should be clear that the problems Congress faces in reforming welfare are inherent in a system that provides highly variable and locally generous benefits under several independent and uncoordinated programs on the basis of geographically variable eligibility. The reason Congress has found it difficult to find a plan that provides universal bene-

24. The program could be terminated in effect without doing so in fact. One means would be to pay a fraction of cash assistance in food stamps. If the value of the stamps were lower than typical food expenditures, the substitution would have little effect (except for any stigma that attaches to the use of food stamps).

fits at a level regarded as reasonable, that preserves work incentives, and that is not vastly more expensive than President Nixon's proposals is that no such plan exists or can be devised: These objectives are mutually inconsistent.

In this predicament, policy makers might be tempted "to leave bad enough alone." This choice is a chimera. The recent growth of federal housing assistance and the likely provision of subsidized day care for the poor assure that the number of low-income families exposed to several implicit taxes in addition to explicit payroll and income taxes will grow rapidly. The current medicaid notches and spend-downs confront the poor with utterly grotesque choices. If policy makers do not face the work incentive problem it will rapidly get worse.

CHAPTER SIX

Whither Welfare Reform?

The welfare system is a hodgepodge of uncoordinated but inter-acting programs, enacted for diverse motives, each written without regard for most of the others. From the standpoint of recipients, at least, these programs form a system—a very complex and often arbitrary system. A major forward step in thinking about welfare reform would be widespread recognition of this fact and of its implication: Creation of effective work incentives requires simultaneous reform of all major income-tested programs. The committee structure within Congress and the departmental bureaucracy of the executive probably exclude the organizational embodiment of such recognition. A useful compromise among the relevant committees and departments would be specific agreement concerning the "sequence" of assistance, that is, the order in which tax rates will be applied. Housing assistance should be broadened to include all those with incomes too meager to buy acceptable housing, whether or not they choose to live in units constructed under federal housing programs. The formula for medicaid assistance should be revised to remove the unconscionable notches and spend-downs that now operate.

The reforms described in Chapter 5 are based on an "incrementalist" view of the American political process. They suggest major evolutionary changes in existing programs, based on three technical principles. First, the tax rate need not be the same on increases in earnings from longer working hours as on increases from higher hourly wages. A second, related, principle, incorporated in the housing and medical assistance formulas described above, is that the government may subsidize increased expenditures at the same time that higher incomes tend to reduce subsidies.

Third, a number of marginal changes in existing programs are in order. In making them, one criterion should be how well they will facilitate subsequent reform. To reduce the wide disparities in state benefits and administrative practice that pose the most serious obstacle to reform, uniform national standards should be established for defining work-related expenses. At present gross variations in state rules operate to create large differences in the actual benefits. Uniform computational procedures should be established under which benefits would be reduced as earnings rose. Uniform procedures should be adopted regarding the earmarking of cash payments for specific family expenditures.

The history of efforts to reform welfare during the years 1969–72 makes clear that none of the several minorities seeking diverse and inconsistent changes in the present system has the power to impose its will on the others. This predicament emerged most clearly in 1972 when eleventh-hour efforts on the floor of the Senate to enact the House-passed welfare reform proposals contained in H.R. 1, to liberalize them, and to substitute the Long plan for them all failed. Welfare reform will succeed only when a coalition has been organized uniting two or more of the groups. If those who seek more generous and uniform benefits are to succeed, they must win over some of those whose concern over work incentives led them to oppose H.R. 1 and more liberal substitutes.

The evolution of the welfare system depends on far broader considerations than the technical matters examined in this paper: It rests on such issues as how much income should be redistributed and to which income classes, how automatic or discretionary such redistribution should be, who should exercise the discretion. Answers to these questions will define the size of a new public assistance program or whatever replaces the current system.